THE EMPTY CHOCOLATE WRAPPER

ADIS ŽIGA

Copyright © 2025 Adis Ziga

Published by CaryPress International Books
www.CaryPress.com

All rights reserved. No part of this publication may be reproduced, distributed, or transmitted in any form or by any means, including photocopying, recording, or other electronic or mechanical methods, without the prior written permission of the publisher, except in the case of brief quotations embodied in critical reviews and certain other non-commercial uses permitted by copyright law.

DEDICATION

*I dedicate this book to my parents, who gave me the gift
of dreams and the ability to realize them.*

*To all genocide victims who lost their lives in Žepa and Srebrenica.
To all of those who overcome adversity and use it to better themselves
and their communities.*

*To the past that shaped me, the present that nurtures me,
and the future that awaits me.*

ACKNOWLEDGMENTS

Transforming a story into a book is as challenging as it is rewarding—a journey that tests both spirit and resolve.

This book owes its existence to the unwavering support of many remarkable individuals. First and foremost, I am deeply grateful to my parents, Ahmo and Raha Ziga, and my sisters, Mubera and Zilka, along with their families, for their constant encouragement. A special thank you to India Little, whose guidance proved invaluable.

I'm also indebted to my countless friends who championed this project from its inception. Finally, my heartfelt appreciation goes to everyone at CaryPress, particularly Dr. Ana Starns, whose exceptional professionalism and dedication helped bring this book to fruition.

Contents

Preface 1

Chapter 1 – Childhood in Yugoslavia 7

Chapter 2 – Shadows of Change 51

Chapter 3 – The Long Winter 77

Chapter 4 – The Crumbling Sanctuary 95

Chapter 5 – Post Exodus: The Long Walk to Freedom 117

Chapter 6 – The Long Road to Reunion.. 131

Chapter 7 – Reunions and New Beginnings..................................... 141

Chapter 8 – New Horizons 155

Epilogue – From Empty Wrappers to Full Circles 165

About The Author 169

Preface

As I sit down to write this preface, a vivid memory resurfaces: the feeling of holding an empty chocolate wrapper, its contents long gone, yet the scent of sweetness lingering. This simple object, once a rare treat in a time of war, now serves as a powerful metaphor for the story you are about to read – a tale of lost innocence, bittersweet memories, and the enduring human spirit in the face of unimaginable adversity.

"The Empty Chocolate Wrapper: Bosnian War Genocide from the Eyes of Innocence" is not just my story; it is a testament to the countless children who found themselves thrust into the heart of a conflict they could barely comprehend. Like that wrapper, we held onto fragments of our childhood, even as the world around us crumbled into chaos and violence.

My decision to embark on this project was born from a deep-seated need to give voice to those who experienced the Bosnian War through the lens of childhood innocence. For years, these memories lay dormant, much like the empty wrapper tucked away in a forgotten pocket – a reminder of sweeter times amidst the bitterness of war. But as time passed, I realized that these stories – my story, my family's story, my people's story – needed to be unwrapped and shared with the world.

The Bosnian War, which raged from 1992 to 1995, is often relegated to the footnotes of history books. Yet, for those of us who lived through it, it was a cataclysmic event that shattered our world and stripped away our innocence far too soon. The genocide in Srebrenica, where over 8,000 Bosniak men and boys were systematically executed, stands as the bitter climax of this conflict – a stark reminder of the depths of human cruelty and the failures of the international community.

But this memoir is not just a recounting of war and its atrocities. It is, at its core, a story of resilience seen through the eyes of a child. Throughout these pages, you will witness how children, myself included, clung to slivers of normalcy and hope, much like we clung to those rare, empty candy wrappers – talismans of a sweeter world we once knew and hoped to taste again.

As you read, you will walk alongside a young boy navigating a world turned upside down by conflict. You'll experience the fear of hiding from snipers, the pangs of hunger that made even the memory of chocolate a luxury, and the heartbreak of losing loved ones. But you'll also witness moments of unexpected joy, acts of profound kindness, and the unwavering bonds of family and community that provided sweetness in the midst of bitterness.

This journey will take you from the mountains of eastern Bosnia to the streets of Sarajevo, from refugee camps to new beginnings in America. Along the way, you'll meet extraordinary individuals who played pivotal roles in my life – resilient mothers who conjured meals out of nothing, brave fathers who risked everything for a scrap of bread for their children, and countless others whose small acts of courage and compassion made survival not just possible, but meaningful.

My hope is that this book will serve as more than just a historical account or a personal memoir. I want it to be a source of inspiration, a reminder that even in the darkest times, the human spirit – especially that of a child – can find light, hope, and even moments of joy. Through my experiences, I hope you'll find:

1. The power of imagination: How children can create worlds of play and fantasy even in the harshest realities.

2. The strength of innocence: How a child's perspective can sometimes cut through the complexities of war to reveal simple, profound truths.

3. The importance of small pleasures: How something as simple as an empty chocolate wrapper can become a symbol of hope and normality.

4. The resilience of family: How parents and siblings can create a cocoon of love and protection even in the most dangerous circumstances.

5. The endurance of cultural identity: How traditions and beliefs can anchor a child's sense of self even when their world is in chaos.

6. The possibility of healing: How even the deepest wounds of childhood can, with time and care, begin to heal.

This story is also a testament to the resilience of the Bosnian people as a whole, seen through the eyes of its most vulnerable members – its children. Despite facing ethnic cleansing, genocide, and the destruction of their homes and way of life, they have persevered. They have rebuilt their lives, whether in Bosnia or as part of the diaspora spread across the globe, carrying with them the bittersweet memories of a childhood interrupted.

As you read this memoir, I invite you to see beyond the specifics of the Bosnian conflict and recognize the universal experiences of children in war zones around the world. The struggles and triumphs depicted here echo the experiences of young refugees and survivors everywhere, yesterday and today. By understanding one child's story in depth, my hope is that readers will develop greater empathy and awareness for all those who face war, displacement, and the challenge of rebuilding their lives.

Writing this book has been a profound journey of its own. It has required me to revisit painful memories, to unwrap experiences long tucked away, and to view my childhood through the lens of adult understanding. But it has also been an opportunity for healing, for honoring the child I was and the children who didn't survive to tell their stories.

As we stand today, nearly three decades after the end of the Bosnian War, the lessons of this conflict remain painfully relevant. In a world still plagued by conflicts that rob children of their innocence, the story of Bosnia serves as both a warning and a beacon of hope. It reminds us of the terrible consequences of hatred and division, but also of the remarkable capacity of the human spirit – even in its most innocent form – to survive, to find joy, and to build a better future.

So, dear reader, as you turn these pages, I invite you to unwrap this story with the wonder and openness of a child. Allow yourself to feel the fear, the pain, the joy, and the triumph through the eyes of innocence. Let this journey transport you to a time and place where even an empty chocolate wrapper could be a treasure, a reminder of sweetness in a world turned bitter.

Thank you for joining me on this journey of remembrance, resilience, and the enduring power of childhood innocence in the face of unimaginable adversity.

CHAPTER 1

Childhood in Yugoslavia

Playing with My Sisters

"Zilka! Mubera!" I called out for my sisters, my voice echoing through the empty rooms. At two-years-old, my little legs were tall enough to peer slightly over the window sill.

One sunny afternoon, I awoke to the soft chirping of birds outside my window. The house felt unusually quiet, and a pang of loneliness settled in my chest. I tiptoed through the hall, peering into the kitchen and living room, but there was no sign of my sisters.

I wandered over to the window, where the plum and hazelnut trees danced gently in the breeze. Their lush branches framed the view of our small yard and the street beyond. In the distance, I heard the familiar sounds of children laughing and playing. My heart sank—I was missing out on the fun.

I made my way to the enclosed porch, hoping to catch a glimpse of Zilka and Mubera. Sure enough, there they were, outside with the neighborhood kids. I realized they had locked the door to keep me safe while I napped, but now I was wide awake and desperate to join them.

With tiny fists, I banged on the window, my eyes brimming with tears. It didn't take long for them to notice. Zilka, ever the caretaker, rushed over, unlocking the door with an apologetic smile.

"We didn't want to wake you, Adis," she said, pulling me into a warm hug. "But we couldn't leave you alone inside."

I sniffled, feeling both relieved and grateful. Hand in hand, we dashed into the vibrant world of our backyard, where laughter and adventure awaited.

There was a sense of relief knowing Zilka had gotten to me before our mother returned from the fields. If she had found me banging on the window, Zilka would have faced a stern reprimand, something I hated to witness.

Family portrait (from left to right): My father, sisters Mubera and Zilka, and my mother holding me as an infant.

We transformed the woods into a realm of endless possibilities, our imaginations running wild as we played hide and seek among the trees. The forest became our enchanted kingdom, each branch and leaf a part of our magical world.

Zilka, always full of stories, spun tales of mythical creatures that lived in the woods. "Beware of the forest spirits," she'd whisper, her eyes wide with feigned seriousness. "They watch over us, but they love a good game."

Mubera, the daring one, would lead us on expeditions deeper into the thicket, claiming we were explorers uncovering hidden treasures. We'd leap over streams, our laughter mingling with the rustle of leaves and the distant calls of birds. Each adventure brought us closer, strengthening the bond that only siblings could share.

Growing up with my two older sisters meant every day was an adventure. I adored Zilka and Mubera; they were my guides, my protectors, and my partners in crime.

As the sun began to set, casting golden hues across the landscape, we knew it was almost time for Majka, our mother to come home after working all day in the fields. Her work was still not done as she had to prepare dinner and take care of three young ones, as Babo, our father was working in Slovenia for a construction company. We would reluctantly head back inside, our feet dusty from the day's exploits, our hearts full of shared memories.

As the day began to wind down, I found myself perched by the window once again, this time eagerly awaiting my mother's return. The street stretched out before me, a familiar path that led to the fields where she toiled each day. Suddenly, a figure appeared in the distance, and my heart leaped with recognition. It was Majka, her silhouette growing clearer with each step.

But then, something unexpected happened. Majka paused, her attention caught by our neighbor's cow grazing near the road. I watched, fascinated, as she approached the animal with a gentle smile. Her hand reached out, softly petting the cow's head, her fingers running through its coarse fur. What surprised me most was how she leaned in, speaking to the cow in hushed tones as if sharing a secret with an old friend.

This tender scene reminded me of our own beloved cows back home - Sarka, with her striking red and white patterns, and Medulja, whose solid brown coat reminded me of the rich earth in our fields. Majka didn't see them as mere farm animals; to her, they were cherished companions.

I remembered a time when, driven by curiosity, I had tried to feed one of our cows. Its rough, sandpaper-like tongue had startled me as it grasped my small hand. Majka's face had paled with worry, her voice stern as she reminded me of her warnings not to feed the cows alone. But even in her concern, her love for both the animals and me was evident.

As if reading my thoughts, Majka often encouraged us to drink the fresh, raw milk our cows provided. "This is nature's gift," she would say, pouring the creamy liquid into our cups. "It makes you strong and healthy." Her words instilled in us not just an appreciation for the nourishment but also a deep respect for the animals that provided it.

Watching Majka with the neighbor's cow, I understood that her affection extended beyond our own animals. To her, every cow was worthy of kindness and respect. As she finally continued her journey home, I felt a warmth spread through my chest, knowing that the same love she showed these gentle creatures was the love she showered upon us, her children.

Indeed, my mother's love and care extended equally to all her children, including my sisters Zilka and Mubera. While I often felt the warmth of her affection, I came to realize as I grew older that her nurturing nature embraced us all.

Zilka, my older sister, was named after my paternal grandmother - a choice that reflected my mother's respect for family traditions and her desire to strengthen familial bonds. This thoughtful naming was just one example of how my mother showed her love and consideration for all her children.

Mubera, too, received the same level of care and attention. My mother's approach to parenting was consistent - she believed in nurturing our individual strengths while instilling in us the same values of hard work, respect, and resilience.

I remember how my mother would often say, "You are all capable of great things." This encouragement wasn't directed solely at me, but at all of us. She had a way of making each of us feel special and valued, while also teaching us the importance of supporting one another as siblings.

There were times when I'd witness tender moments between my mother and my sisters - helping Zilka with her studies, teaching Mubera how to cook traditional Bosnian dishes, or simply offering a listening ear when they needed to talk. These interactions showed me that my mother's love was boundless, encompassing all her children with equal fervor.

Looking back, I realize that my mother's affection and guidance shaped not just me, but all of us, preparing us for the challenges that lay ahead and binding us together as a family unit. Her love was a constant, a foundation upon which we all built our lives.

To this day, I have utmost respect and love for both of our parents, who were able to build something out of nothing and provide for this family.

The Bookmark

One sunny afternoon, I found myself in our small living room, my precious chocolate wrapper clutched in my tiny hands. I had been carrying it around for days, much to my mother's amusement and mild concern.

Zilka sat cross-legged on the floor, surrounded by her schoolbooks. Her long dark hair was tied back in a neat braid, and her brow furrowed in concentration as she pored over her studies.

"Zilka," I called, toddling over to her. "Look!"

I proudly held out my prized possession - the empty chocolate wrapper, its bright colors now slightly faded, its edges worn soft from constant handling.

Zilka looked up, a gentle smile spreading across her face. "Oh, Adis," she laughed, "are you still carrying that around?"

I nodded vigorously, clutching the wrapper closer to my chest.

"You know," Zilka said thoughtfully, "I have an idea. Why don't we make something special with your wrapper?"

My eyes widened with curiosity. "Special?"

Zilka nodded, her eyes twinkling. "Yes, something very special. A bookmark!"

She carefully took the wrapper from my hands and smoothed it out on her textbook. Then, with practiced movements, she began to fold it, transforming the flat piece of foil into a long, narrow strip.

"See?" she said, holding up her creation. "Now you can keep your treasure forever, and it can help me keep my place in my books."

I clapped my hands in delight, marveling at the magic my sister had performed. The wrapper, once just a memento of a long-gone treat, was now something useful, something important.

Zilka slipped the new bookmark into her textbook and pulled me into a warm hug. "There," she said, "now a little piece of you will always be with me when I study."

From that day on, whenever I saw Zilka with her books, I would look for that glint of colorful foil peeking out from between the pages. It was our secret, a symbol of the bond we shared, and a reminder that even the simplest things could be transformed into something precious with a little love and creativity.

Little did I know then how that small act of turning something discarded into something cherished would echo throughout my life, especially in the difficult years to come.

The Walk

The next day, my mother had planned a visit. Before stepping out of the house, one of the enduring memories of my childhood is my mother's gentle reminder each time we left the house: "Adis, make sure you step out with your right foot first."

This wasn't just a random instruction, but a deeply ingrained cultural and religious practice that my mother passed down to us. In Islamic tradition, starting things with the right side is considered auspicious and blessed. My mother extended this to literally starting our day on the right foot.

"*Bismillah*[1]," she would whisper, reminding us to say the name of Allah as we took that first step out the door. It was more than just a superstition; it was a way of setting intention for the day ahead.

As I grew older, I began to understand the deeper significance of this simple act. Stepping out with the right foot became a physical manifestation of positive thinking, a daily affirmation that we were starting our day in the best possible way.

My mother's wisdom didn't stop there. She had a whole routine of positive practices to start the day:

"Put on your right sock first, then your left," she'd instruct. "When you put on your shoes, start with the right foot too."

These small acts were like a ritual, a way of mindfully beginning each day with purpose and positivity. It was as if each right-footed step was a small prayer, a hope for a good day ahead.

Now, as an adult, I see how these childhood lessons align with modern concepts of positive affirmations and mindfulness. My mother, in her traditional wisdom, was teaching us to start each day with intention, to literally and figuratively put our best foot forward.

This practice has stayed with me, a comforting routine that connects me to my roots and reminds me of my mother's loving guidance. Even now,

---

[1] Translates to "In the name of Allah" in English. It is often used by Muslims before beginning an action or task, as a way to invoke blessings and guidance from God.

thousands of miles from my childhood home, I find myself unconsciously starting my day on the right foot, carrying with me that small piece of my mother's wisdom and love.

It's a beautiful reminder that sometimes, the most profound life lessons come wrapped in the simplest of instructions. My mother's insistence on starting with the right foot was her way of teaching us to approach each day with optimism, mindfulness, and faith - lessons that have served me well throughout my life.

The cobblestones clicked beneath my small feet as I walked hand-in-hand with my mother through the winding streets of Žepa. It was early summer, and the air was thick with the scent of blooming plum trees. I was barely four years old, dressed in a matching short-sleeved shirt and shorts that my mother had carefully chosen for our walk to visit my grandparents.

"*Pazi, sine*[2]," my mother cautioned gently to watch out, "be careful not to kick the rocks. You'll damage your shoes and hurt your feet."

I nodded, trying to resist the temptation of the rhythmic sound they made as they skipped away. My mother – my *majka* – was a frugal woman, and I knew her words came from a place of both love and practicality. In our small Bosnian town, nestled in the heart of Yugoslavia, every resource was precious.

The village of Štitkov Do stretched before us, quaint and familiar. As we walked, the familiar sights of our community unfolded around us. Žepa was a modest place, home to only a few thousand souls, but to me, it was the entire world. The houses, built of sturdy stone by generations of

---

[2] Translates to "Be careful, son."

masons, stood proudly on either side of the street. On one side, homes where families had lived for decades; on the other, stalls for livestock and storage.

My mother seemed to know everyone we passed. She would pause to exchange greetings, her voice a melody of warmth and respect.

"*Selam alejkum*[3]," she would say, and I would echo her words, feeling grown-up and important.

"Salam!!" neighbors would call out, waving warmly. "How are the children?"

"They're well, Alhamdulillah[4]," she'd reply, squeezing my hand. "And how is your family?"

As we continued our journey, I admired the fields and wooden fences adorned with wildflowers. The air was sweet with the scent of blooming flora, a reminder that spring had embraced the land. Each step brought us closer to our destination, my grandparents' home, nestled on a hill overlooking the village.

My mother would often point out the vibrant tapestry of wildflowers lining the path, naming each one with care. "These are poppies, Adis," she'd say, her voice filled with reverence. "They remind us of the beauty that can thrive even in the harshest conditions."

I'd nod, entranced by the vivid colors and delicate petals. These walks with my mother were more than just journeys to a destination; they were

---

[3] Translates to "Peace be upon you" in English. It is a common greeting in Arabic and among Muslims.
[4] Praise be to God: said as a way to show gratitude for the blessings.

lessons in appreciating the simple joys of life, in finding beauty in the everyday.

As we approached, the road inclined, and I spotted the little red-roofed house. Excitement bubbled within me, knowing we were almost there. I squinted, following her gesture. There, perched on the hill ahead of us, was the familiar red roof of my grandparents' home. The sight filled me with excitement and a touch of relief – my legs were growing tired from our journey. "Look, Majka!" I exclaimed, pointing eagerly. "We're close!" I squinted, following her gesture. There, perched on the hill ahead of us, was the familiar red roof of my grandparents' home. The sight filled me with excitement and a touch of relief – my legs were growing tired from our journey.

"Yes, we are," she said, her eyes twinkling with affection. "But first, the fountain."

We stopped at the village fountain, where crystal-clear water gushed from the earth. My mother took a sip, then held her hands under the stream, letting the cool water trickle through her fingers. I mimicked her, savoring the refreshing sensation on my palms. It was a small ritual, one I cherished, that connected us to the land of water—our Bosnia.

The fountain was more than just a place to quench our thirst; it was a symbol of community, a gathering spot where villagers shared stories and laughter. I loved listening to the tales of old, passed down through generations, each one weaving a tapestry of history and culture.

As we continued our ascent, I became distracted by the unusual stones lining the road. They were unlike anything I'd seen before – red and porous, almost like volcanic rock. I couldn't resist reaching down to touch one, marveling at its rough texture.

"Those are pumice stones," my mother explained, noticing my fascination. "They're special, just like our town."

I nodded, filing away this new piece of knowledge. Everything about Žepa felt special to me – the stones, the trees, the people. It was a place where three cultures – Bosniak, Serbian, and Croatian – lived side by side in harmony. Though I was too young to fully understand the complexities of our multicultural society, I could feel the richness of it in the air around me.

As we approached the cemetery that marked the final stretch of our journey, my mother's demeanor changed subtly. She reached into her bag and pulled out a headscarf, shaking it out before carefully draping it over her hair. I watched, transfixed, as she transformed before my eyes – not into someone different, but into a more formal version of herself.

"We're going to say a prayer for Dedo (pronounced as Jedo[5]) Ago as well as the rest of the family," she said softly, referring to my maternal grandfather who had passed away before I was born.

I nodded solemnly, understanding the importance of this ritual even if I couldn't fully grasp its meaning. We paused at the entrance to the cemetery, and my mother's lips moved in silent prayer. I tried to mimic her reverent expression, feeling a connection to something greater than myself.

---

[5] Grandfather

The next mini-stop on our journey was at the home of Mr. Latif, an elderly family friend who lived in a quaint cottage at the edge of town. His small house was surrounded by a vibrant garden, but the true treasure lay behind it - several rows of white wooden beehives.

Mr. Latif was a skilled beekeeper, tending to his hives with a gentleness that belied his weathered hands. Whenever we visited, he would greet us with a warm smile that crinkled the corners of his eyes. The scent of honey and beeswax always clung to his clothes, a sweet reminder of his passion.

The highlight of each visit was when Mr. Latif would reach into a glass jar on his kitchen counter and offer me a piece of homemade honey candy. These golden, translucent treats were hard and smooth, melting slowly on my tongue to release their rich, floral sweetness. Each piece was a labor of love, crafted from the honey produced by his own bees.

As I savored the candy, Mr. Latif would often regale us with stories of his beekeeping adventures or share fascinating facts about the intricate lives of bees. Those moments in his cozy kitchen, surrounded by the gentle humming from the nearby hives, remain some of my fondest childhood memories.

As we resumed our walk, the sound of laughter and shouts drifted down from my grandparents' house. My spirits lifted immediately – I recognized the voices of my cousins, playing with their friends.

"Majka," I tugged at my mother's hand. "Can I go play with my cousins when we get there?"

My mother smiled down at me, her eyes crinkling at the corners. "We'll see, sine. First, we must greet your nana and help her with any chores she might have."

I nodded, trying to hide my impatience. At four years old, I was the baby of the family, doted on by my parents and sisters alike. But I longed to be big enough to join in their games and adventures.

As we finally crested the hill and my grandparents' house came fully into view, I felt a surge of excitement. This place, with its weathered stone walls and welcoming door, was a second home to me. It represented family, love, and the simple joys of life in our small corner of Bosnia.

Little did I know that the peaceful world I knew – a world of cobblestone streets, family visits, and the intermingling of cultures – was more fragile than I could have imagined. The year was 1987, and storm clouds were gathering on the horizon of Yugoslavia. But for now, in this moment, there was only the warmth of the sun, the love of family, and the promise of a day filled with simple pleasures in Žepa.

The Day I Was Born

The day of my birth in 1983, was not an ordinary day. My mother often recounted the story of my birth, painting a vivid picture of the unexpected arrival. I was born in the back of a car, somewhere between Žepa and Rogatica, surrounded by towering pine trees. Majka always said that the trees blessed me, their strength and height a gift from nature, as currently I'm 6' 4'.

"It's why you're so tall," she'd tease, a playful glint in her eye. "Born under the sun and among the giants."

My birth was anything but ordinary. While my father was away working in Slovenia, my mother and aunt Mina, my father's sister, began the long journey to the hospital. But I had other plans. As their car wound through the dense forest between Žepa and Rogatica, I decided it was time to enter the world. There in the backseat, with only the towering pine trees as witnesses, my aunt helped my mother deliver me. Using a pocket knife, she cut the umbilical cord and tied it with a string hastily pulled from her own blouse. Only afterward did we finally reach the hospital in Rogatica.

My mother would often tell me about the peacocks that sang outside the hospital window all night, their vibrant displays a celebration of my arrival. "It was as if the world knew you were special," she'd say. "A good omen, a sign of the great things you would achieve."

The story of my birth became a cherished tale in our family, a reminder of the unpredictable beauty of life. My mother's strength and resilience shone through that day, qualities she instilled in me as I grew.

I often imagined the towering pine trees, their branches swaying in the wind, welcoming me into the world. They stood as silent guardians, witnesses to my first breath, their roots intertwined with the soil of my homeland. This connection to nature, to the land of Bosnia, became an integral part of my identity.

My name, Adis, carries a unique story that began before I was even born. It was my father who chose it, long before ultrasounds were common for revealing a baby's gender. His choice was inspired by a memorable experience during his time working as a construction foreman in Slovenia.

In the early 1980s, my father had taken a job overseeing a large building project in Ljubljana. The work was challenging, with long hours and a language barrier to navigate. But amidst the chaos of the construction site, there was one constant source of help and positivity - a local boy named Adis.

Adis, no more than twelve or thirteen, would often appear after school, eager to lend a hand. He'd run errands, translate conversations with local workers, and even assist with small tasks on the site. What struck my father most was Adis's impeccable behavior and unwavering helpfulness. In a high-stress environment, the young lad's presence was a breath of fresh air.

My father never forgot Adis or his impact. So when it came time to name his own child, he decided that if he had a son, he would name him after this exemplary boy he had met in Slovenia. The name would serve as a tribute to the qualities he admired: diligence, helpfulness, and good character.

As it turned out, I was indeed a boy, and my parents followed through with my father's wish. Growing up, I often heard the story behind my name, and it instilled in me a sense of the values my father hoped I'd embody. In a way, my name became not just a label, but a legacy connecting me to a place I'd never been and a boy I'd never met, but whose impact had reached across continents and generations.

The Olympic Pride of Yugoslavia

In 1984, a year after I was born, Yugoslavia hosted the Winter Olympic Games in Sarajevo. Though I was too young to remember the event itself, the pride and excitement it brought to our country lingered for years, becoming a part of our collective memory.

"Can you believe it, Adis?" my father would say, his eyes shining with pride. "Our Bosnia, out of all the republics, was chosen to host the Olympics. The whole world was watching us!"

I'd listen, wide-eyed, as my parents recounted tales of the newly built hotels, the pristine ski slopes, and the state-of-the-art bobsled track. The Games had put Yugoslavia on the global map, showcasing our ability to organize a world-class event.

As I grew older, I'd pore over books and magazines, marveling at the images of the Olympic venues. "One day," I'd whisper to myself, "I'll visit all these places."

Little did I know then that these symbols of national pride would later become silent witnesses to a darker chapter in our history.

Summer Days and Homemade Delights

The long summer days in Žepa were filled with the sweet scent of ripening fruit and the excitement of preserving nature's bounty. One of my fondest memories is of the jam-making process, a community affair that brought neighbors together under the starry sky.

"Adis, come help us with the plums!" my mother called one warm evening.

I ran to join her and the other women of the village gathered around an enormous copper pot called a bakrač. It could hold 40-50 gallons and was perched over a roaring fire at the top of our village.

As night fell, the air filled with laughter and the rich aroma of simmering fruit. We children darted between the adults, sneaking tastes of the sweet concoction when we thought no one was looking.

"Careful," my mother would warn with a smile. "It's still hot!"

We'd stay up until nearly midnight, mesmerized by the hypnotic stirring of the jam and the stories shared around the fire. It was more than just making preserves; it was about preserving our way of life, our connections to each other and to the land.

The Gypsy Merchants and Childhood Fears

The arrival of the Roma merchants in our village was always an event filled with excitement and a touch of fear. Their colorful caravans would roll into town, bringing with them an array of copper wares, brushes, and other goods.

"Majka, the gypsies are here!" I'd exclaim, peering out the window with a mix of curiosity and trepidation.

My mother would nod seriously. "Remember, Adis, behave yourself. You know what happens to naughty children when the gypsies come."

It was a common threat among parents in our village - misbehaving children might be snatched away by the Roma. Of course, it was just a tale to keep us in line, but as a child, the fear felt very real.

Despite the warnings, I couldn't help but be fascinated by these nomadic people. Their lives seemed so different from ours, full of adventure and mystery. As I grew older, I began to understand the prejudices behind these warnings, but the memory of those visits remained a vivid part of my childhood.

The Fabric of Tradition: Dimije

In our village, the arrival of textile merchants was always an event that stirred excitement among the women. These visits were particularly special for my sisters Zilka and Mubera, as they offered a glimpse into the intricate world of traditional Bosnian clothing, especially the dimije.

One warm afternoon, Zilka and Mubera watched as our mother and the other women of the village gathered around a merchant's colorful display of fabrics. Their eyes sparkled with anticipation as they ran their hands over the various textures and patterns.

"Zilka, Mubera, come here," our mother called, waving them over. "What do you think of this one?"

She held up a length of fabric adorned with intricate floral designs. My sisters nodded enthusiastically, always in awe of our mother's ability to envision the final garment from a simple piece of cloth. Later on, both sisters transitioned into more modern attire they would see at school.

"This will make a beautiful dimije," she said, her eyes twinkling. "And look at these patterns! You'll always be able to spot me in a crowd."

Zilka and Mubera smiled, understanding the practical wisdom behind her choice. In a sea of women wearing dimije, our mother's vibrant patterns would stand out, making it easy for them to find her at gatherings or in the marketplace.

The dimije, my sisters learned, was more than just a piece of clothing. It was a symbol of our cultural heritage, a garment that had clothed generations of Bosnian women. Unlike the simple skirts they'd seen in pictures of other countries, the dimije was a pair of voluminous pants that billowed out like a skirt, offering both modesty and practicality.

As our mother carefully selected her fabrics, she explained the art of making dimije to Zilka and Mubera. "You see, girls," she said, "the dimije allows us to move freely while working in the fields or around the house. It's cool in summer and warm in winter."

My sisters watched in fascination as the women discussed different styles and patterns. Some preferred solid colors, but our mother always gravitated towards the bold, distinctive designs. "It's not just about looking pretty," she'd say with a wink. "It's about making sure my little girls can always find me."

"When I was your age," our grandmother chimed in, her eyes misty with memories, "every young woman learned to sew her own dimije. It was a rite of passage."

As the years passed, Zilka and Mubera noticed fewer young women wearing dimije, opting instead for more modern styles. But our mother and many of the older women in our village continued to wear them with pride, a living connection to our past.

Looking back, my sisters realized that those moments around the merchant's wares were more than just about choosing fabrics. They were lessons in our culture, our history, and the quiet strength of the women who kept our traditions alive. The dimije, with its flowing lines and practical design, became a symbol in their minds of the grace and resilience of Bosnian women, a legacy carried in every stitch and fold. And for Zilka and Mubera, those bright patterns our mother chose were a beacon, a familiar sight that always led them home in a crowd.

The Influence of Family

Family was the cornerstone of my upbringing. My grandparents' home, perched on the hill, was a haven of love and warmth. My grandmother, with her gentle smile and soothing voice, would envelop us in her embrace, her apron perpetually dusted with flour from her endless baking.

She was the keeper of our family's traditions, passing down recipes and stories that had been cherished for generations. In her kitchen, the aroma of freshly baked bread mingled with the scent of herbs from her garden. Each meal was a celebration, a feast that brought us together, reinforcing the bonds that held our family close.

My grandfather, a man of few words but endless wisdom, would regale us with tales of his youth. His eyes sparkled with mischief as he shared stories of his adventures, each one a lesson in resilience and courage. He taught me the value of hard work, the importance of integrity, and the beauty of living in harmony with nature.

Our family gatherings were filled with laughter and music, the sounds of traditional Bosnian songs echoing through the air. My aunts and uncles would join in, their voices blending in perfect harmony, creating a symphony that resonated deep within my soul. These moments, etched in my memory, shaped my understanding of love, community, and belonging.

The Steadfast Faith of Nana Behija

My maternal grandmother, Behija

My maternal grandmother, Behija, was a pillar of unwavering faith and tradition in our family. Unlike my paternal grandmother who lived in the bustling city of Sarajevo, Nana Behija was deeply rooted in our village life and its customs.

"Bismillah," I would hear her whisper softly as she began any task, no matter how small. This simple phrase, "In the name of Allah," was a constant reminder of her deep and abiding faith.

Nana Behija was never without her hijab, the traditional headscarf worn by Muslim women. To my young eyes, it seemed as much a part of her as her gentle smile or her warm, comforting hands. The hijab wasn't just a piece of clothing to her; it was a symbol of her devotion, a visible expression of her faith.

One of my most vivid memories of Nana Behija was her dedication to reading the Quran. It seemed that whenever I visited her, I would find her sitting on her balcony, legs crossed, with the holy book open before her. Her voice, soft but clear, would carry the melodic recitations of the verses on the breeze.

"Adis," she would call to me, her eyes twinkling, "come, sit with me. Let's read together."

Those moments on the balcony, listening to her recite and trying my best to follow along, instilled in me a deep respect for our religious traditions. Even when I didn't fully understand the words, the peace and contentment on her face as she read left a lasting impression.

Another distinctive feature of Nana Behija was her hands, always stained with henna. The reddish-brown dye wasn't just for decoration; it was a part of her daily life, applied regularly for its believed medicinal properties and as a sign of cultural tradition.

"See, Adis," she would say, holding out her hands for me to inspect, "the henna protects and heals. It's Allah's gift to us."

Nana Behija's influence extended beyond just religious teachings. She was a keeper of our family's history and traditions. From her, I learned about our ancestors, the struggles they had faced, and the values that had sustained our family through generations.

Her kitchen was always a hub of activity, filled with the aroma of traditional Bosnian dishes. She took great pride in passing down recipes and cooking techniques to my mother and aunts, ensuring that our culinary heritage would continue.

"Food nourishes more than just the body," she would often say. "It feeds the soul and keeps our traditions alive."

Even as the world around us changed, Nana Behija remained a constant, a living link to our past. Her unwavering faith, her dedication to tradition, and her boundless love for her family shaped not just my childhood, but the very fabric of who I am.

Looking back now, I realize how fortunate I was to have had such a strong and devoted grandmother. Nana Behija's legacy lives on in the values she instilled in us, in the traditions we continue to practice, and in the faith that guides us. Her life was a testament to the power of belief, the importance of heritage, and the enduring strength of a grandmother's love.

The Silent Strength of Dedo (pronounced as Jedo) Ismet

Among the figures who loomed large in my childhood memories, my grandfather Ismet held a special place. He was a man of few words, but his presence spoke volumes, embodying the quiet strength and traditional values that were the bedrock of our family.

I remember him most vividly in his later years, a tall figure dressed in traditional Bosnian clothing, his head adorned with a distinctive turban. This attire wasn't just clothing to him; it was a statement of identity, a link to our cultural heritage that he wore with quiet pride.

"Your jedo Ismet," my father would tell me, "he's a man who's seen much in his life."

Indeed, grandfather Ismet had lived through tumultuous times. He had witnessed the fall of empires, the redrawing of borders, and the changing face of our homeland. Yet through it all, he remained a constant, unchanging presence, like a sturdy oak tree weathering storm after storm.

What I remember most about him was not so much what he said, but how he was. He moved with a deliberate slowness, each action seeming to carry the weight of careful consideration. When he did speak, his words were few but meaningful, often imparting some piece of wisdom or insight that would stay with me long after.

I recall sitting at his feet as a young boy, listening intently as he shared stories from his youth. Though the details of these tales have faded with time, the feeling of connection to our family's past remains vivid. It was as if, through his words, he was passing down not just stories, but a piece of our identity.

One memory stands out clearly - the day grandfather Ismet passed away. I was young, perhaps three or four years old, but I sensed the gravity of the moment. The house was filled with a solemn quiet, broken only by soft prayers and muffled sobs.

"He was harvesting gravel," my father explained to me later, his voice thick with emotion. "It was an accident."

I didn't fully understand then what harvesting gravel meant or how dangerous it could be. But I knew that my grandfather, this pillar of strength in our family, was gone. It was my first real encounter with loss, a moment that marked the end of one chapter in our family's story and the beginning of another.

In the years that followed, grandfather Ismet's memory lived on in our family's stories and traditions. The values he embodied - hard work, quiet dignity, and unwavering faith - continued to shape our family long after he was gone.

Looking back now, I realize how fortunate I was to have known him, even for a short time. Grandfather Ismet was more than just a relative; he was a living link to our past, a guardian of our traditions, and a model of the kind of person I could aspire to be.

His life and his passing taught me important lessons about the cycle of life, the value of our cultural heritage, and the quiet strength that can reside in a person. Though he spoke little, his actions and his very being left an indelible mark on our family, shaping us in ways we're still discovering to this day.

A Stand Against Tyranny: My Great-Grandfather's Bravery

Among the many stories passed down through our family, one tale stood out for its raw courage and defiance in the face of great danger. It was the story of my great-grandfather, Šaćir (pronounced as Shakir), a man whose bravery during World War II became a source of pride for generations to come.

"Your great-grandfather was a tall, strong man," my mother would say, her eyes distant with memory. "They say you look just like him, Adis. Blonde hair, tall stature - but it's his courage I hope you've inherited."

The story took place during the dark days of World War II when the Chetniks, Serbian nationalist and royalist paramilitary groups, were terrorizing Muslim villages throughout Bosnia. These were times of fear and uncertainty, when the knock on a door could mean life or death.

One day, a group of Četnik (pronounced as Chetniks) arrived at the outskirts of our village. Word spread quickly, and panic began to set in. But while others trembled, my great-grandfather Šaćir stood tall.

"He didn't have any weapons," my mother would explain, her voice filled with awe. "He had nothing but his courage and his words."

As the story goes, Šaćir walked out to meet the Chetniks. He stood before them, unarmed and alone, a solitary figure facing a group of armed men.

"This is our home," he reportedly said, his voice steady and strong. "You cannot pass. We have done you no harm, and we will not allow you to harm us."

The Chetniks, surprised by this display of bravery, hesitated. Here was a man, alone and unarmed, daring to stand against them. In that moment of hesitation, Šaćir continued to speak, appealing to their humanity, reminding them that Muslims, Serbs, and Croats had lived side by side in peace for generations.

"We are all people of this land," he said. "Why should we fight each other when we could live as neighbors?"

Whether it was the power of his words, the strength of his conviction, or simply the shock of encountering such unexpected resistance, the Chetniks withdrew. They left the village untouched, and Šaćir's act of courage saved not just his family, but the entire community.

This story was more than just a tale of bravery; it was a lesson in standing up for what's right, in the power of words over weapons, and in the importance of seeing humanity in others, even in our enemies.

As I grew older, I often thought about my great-grandfather Šaćir. I wondered if I would have the same courage if faced with such a situation. His story became a touchstone for me, a reminder of the strength that runs in our family's blood.

"Remember," my mother would say, "bravery isn't about being fearless. It's about doing what's right even when you're afraid. That's what your great-grandfather did that day."

In a world that often seemed chaotic and unpredictable, the story of my great-grandfather's stand against the Chetniks was a beacon of hope. It showed that one person, armed with nothing but conviction and courage, could make a difference. It was a legacy of bravery that I hoped to live up to, a reminder that in the darkest of times, we always have a choice to stand up for what's right.

Eid al-Adha: The Feast of Sacrifice

As the summer sun rose over the hills of Žepa, there was a palpable excitement in the air. It was the morning of Eid al-Adha, one of the most important holidays in our Muslim calendar. The entire village buzzed with activity as families prepared for the day of celebration and remembrance.

"Zilka, Mubera, Adis!" my father called out. "Come, it's time."

We gathered in the yard where a young ram stood tethered to a post. Its wool was clean and white, having been carefully tended for this very day. My father approached it with a mixture of reverence and purpose.

"Children," he said softly, "do you remember the story of Prophet Ibrahim?"

We nodded solemnly. Every year, he would retell the tale of Ibrahim's unwavering faith and his willingness to sacrifice his son at Allah's command.

And every year, the story filled me with awe.

"This sacrifice," my father continued, gesturing to the ram, "is our way of honoring Ibrahim's devotion and Allah's mercy."

As he prepared for the sacrifice, I noticed the special care he took. He sharpened his knife meticulously, explaining, "We must ensure the animal feels as little pain as possible. This is not just tradition; it's about compassion."

My sisters and I watched as he whispered a prayer and gently calmed the animal. It was a solemn moment, filled with a deep sense of connection to our faith and our ancestors who had performed this ritual for generations.

After the sacrifice, the real work began. Nothing would be wasted. My mother and aunts busied themselves preparing the meat, much of which would be distributed to those in need.

"Remember," my mother said as she handed us packages to deliver to our neighbors, "Eid is about sharing our blessings."

The rest of the day was filled with visits to family and friends, the air rich with the aroma of roasting meat and sweet pastries. We children, dressed in our best clothes, ran from house to house, collecting treats and small gifts.

As the sun set, our family gathered for the feast. The table was laden with dishes made from the sacrificial lamb – succulent roasts, hearty stews, and my favorite, the savory pies my mother made.

Looking around at the smiling faces of my family, I felt a profound sense of belonging. Eid al-Adha was more than just a holiday; it was a reminder of our faith, our community, and the importance of compassion and giving.

That night, as I drifted off to sleep, my belly full and my heart content, I reflected on the day's events. The sacrifice, which had once seemed scary to my younger self, now represented something beautiful – a testament to faith, tradition, and the enduring bonds of family and community.

Summer Adventures in an Empty Village

As the scorching summer heat descended upon Žepa, a curious transformation would take place in our village. Many of our neighbors, those with large herds of livestock, would embark on their annual migration to the cooler mountain pastures. For three to four months, they'd relocate their entire households, including chickens and other animals, to their log cabins high in the Bosnian mountains.

For those of us left behind, like my sisters Zilka and Mubera and me, this mass exodus created a playground like no other.

"Look!" I'd shout excitedly to my sisters. "The Štitkovac family just left. Their yard is ours now!"

Zilka, always the voice of reason, would caution, "Remember, Adis, we can't actually go inside their houses."

But Mubera, with a mischievous glint in her eye, would add, "But their yards, their sheds, their chicken coops – those are fair game!"

And so, our summer adventures would begin. The once bustling village transformed into a vast, secret playground for us children. Where once we heard stern warnings of "Don't step on my grass!" or "Don't pull down the branches!", now there was only the sound of our laughter echoing through the near-empty streets.

We'd play elaborate games of hide-and-seek, ducking behind abandoned chicken coops or crouching in the tall grass of untended gardens. The entire village became our stage for imaginary adventures.

"I'll hide in the Čavćić's cherry orchard!" Mubera would announce, darting off before Zilka had finished counting.

I'd find my own hiding spot, perhaps behind the woodpile in Hodžić's yard, holding my breath as Zilka searched, her footsteps crunching on the sun-dried grass.

Sometimes, we'd indulge in small acts of mischief, sampling cherries from unattended orchards or peeking into the windows of empty houses, our curiosity getting the better of us. But we were always careful not to cause any real damage or disturbance. After all, these were still our neighbors' homes, even if they were temporarily abandoned.

As the sun began to set, painting the sky in brilliant oranges and pinks, we'd reluctantly make our way home, our pockets bulging with pilfered fruit, our clothes dusty from our adventures.

"Remember," Zilka would remind us as we approached our house, "not a word to Majka about where we've been playing."

We'd nod solemnly, knowing that while our mother might suspect, it was better not to confirm her suspicions. These summer days, with their secret adventures in the empty village, were our special treasure.

Looking back now, I realize how unique those summers were. In those empty yards and quiet streets, we found a freedom that seems almost unimaginable today. It was a time of innocence and adventure, where the boundaries between yards blurred and the entire village truly became one big family home.

Those summers taught us about trust – the trust our community had in each other to respect their absent neighbors' properties. They taught us about the rhythms of rural life, the ebb and flow of seasons that dictated the movements of people and animals. But most of all, they gave us memories of carefree days, filled with laughter and discovery, that would stay with us long after we'd grown and the village had changed.

The Pioneers: Tito's Young Guard

In this photo from my first grade year, I'm with Tito's Pioneers. You can find me in the front row, second from the right, squatting down with blond hair and wearing a green vest.

At the age of seven, my first day of school was more than just the beginning of my education; it marked my induction into the Pioneers, the youth organization that embodied the ideals of Yugoslav socialism.

As always, my mother walked me to the door. Before I left, she kissed me on the cheek, a ritual that had become sacred between us. I never wiped away her kiss; instead, I carried the sensation of her lips on my cheek like a talisman throughout the day.

As I set off on my journey through the forest to school, a trek of three to four kilometers, I felt the warmth of her love with every step. It was as if she had given me a little hug that lasted the entire day, soothing any fears or doubts that might arise.

Looking back, I marvel at my mother's bravery. Sending a child of six or seven to walk alone through the forest would be unthinkable for many parents today. But in our community, it was a normal part of life, a way to instill independence in children. Still, I know it couldn't have been easy for her.

That kiss, that daily gesture of affection, became a bridge between us, easing the separation anxiety for both mother and child. It was a reminder of the strong bond we shared, a bond that would be tested in the years to come as our world changed around us.

These sweet memories of life before the war, of a mother's love expressed in the simplest of gestures, would become precious to me in later years. They were a reminder of a time when our biggest concerns were school and Pioneer meetings, before we knew how fragile peace could be.

At school, the ceremony was about to begin. "Stand tall, Adis," my mother had said as she adjusted my white shirt. "Today, you become part of something bigger than yourself."

The ceremony was a mix of solemnity and excitement. Older Pioneers, including my sister's generation, presided over the event. With trembling hands, I received my blue cap adorned with a red star and the red scarf that would mark me as one of Tito's young guards.

"I..." my voice wavered as I began the oath, then grew stronger, "...as a Pioneer, give my Pioneer's word of honor that I will study and work diligently, respect my parents and my elders, and be a loyal and honest comrade and friend, that I will love our self-managed homeland, the Socialist Federal Republic of Yugoslavia, and that I will dedicate my life to the ideals of peace and socialism."

As I spoke these words, I felt a sense of belonging, of being part of a grand vision that stretched far beyond our small village. Little did I know that I would be among the last to take this oath, as the winds of change were already stirring across our land.

The Strict Teacher and the Hotel Errand

My first-grade teacher, an Orthodox lady who had taught generations of children in our village, was known for her strictness. Her classroom was the only one with pristine green desktops, not a single scratch marring their surface.

"Adis," she called one day, her voice stern but not unkind. "I have an important task for you."

My heart raced as she handed me some money and instructions. I was to go to the hotel down the street and pick up her lunch order. It was a big responsibility for a small boy, and I felt both terrified and proud.

As I stepped into the hotel, the bustling environment overwhelmed me. Adults towered over me, their conversations a confusing buzz. With shaking hands, I approached the counter.

"E-excuse me," I stammered. "I'm here to pick up my teacher's order."

The man behind the counter smiled kindly. "Ah, yes. Here you go, young man."

Carefully balancing the tray with a plate of food and a glass of Coca-Cola, I made my way back to school. The carbonated drink fizzed temptingly, but I resisted the urge to take a sip.

When I returned, my teacher's eyes twinkled. "Well done, Adis. I see you didn't drink any of my Coca-Cola."

I blinked in surprise. "How did you know?"

She just smiled mysteriously, leaving me to wonder at her seemingly magical powers of deduction. It was moments like these that taught me the value of trust and responsibility, lessons that would shape my character in the years to come.

The Yellow Yugo and Visits from Croatia

The arrival of my aunt and her family from Pula, Croatia was always a cause for celebration. Their visits brought a taste of the wider world to our small village.

"Look, Adis!" my sister would shout. "Uncle's yellow Yugo is coming up the road!"

The Yugo, a point of national pride as Yugoslavia's homegrown car, seemed almost exotic to us. As it pulled up, my cousins would tumble out, their speech peppered with a slightly different dialect that marked them as city kids.

"Tell us about the Colosseum!" I'd beg, eager to hear about the ancient Roman amphitheater in their hometown.

These visits were a window into a world beyond Žepa, sparking dreams of travel and adventure in my young mind. Little did I know then that one day, I'd be the one bringing stories of far-off places to my family.

A Tale of Two Worlds: The Divorce That Shaped My Curiosity

The story of my paternal grandparents' divorce was like a faint echo from a distant past, an event that occurred long before I was born but whose repercussions shaped my family dynamics and my own understanding of the world.

"Your grandfather and grandmother separated when your father was just a boy," my mother once told me, her voice soft with a mixture of sympathy and something I couldn't quite place. "It wasn't common back then, especially not in our small village."

I learned that my grandmother had moved to Sarajevo, the bustling capital of Bosnia, leaving behind my grandfather and their children, including my father who was only about 12 at the time. The divorce created a rift in the family, one that took years to mend.

As a child, I struggled to understand this concept. In our close-knit village of Žepa, where tradition and family ties were the bedrock of society, the idea of a broken family seemed almost foreign. Yet, here was this story, part of my own family history, that spoke of a different world, a different way of life.

My paternal grandmother, Zilka, became an enigma to me. She was the modern one, with her permed hair and city clothes, so different from my maternal grandmother who always wore a hijab and traditional Bosnian attire. Zilka's life in Sarajevo seemed like something out of a storybook -

tall, gray communist-era buildings reaching towards the sky, busy streets, and a way of life so different from our rural existence.

My paternal grandmother, Zilka

"Your grandmother lives on the 5th floor," my mother would say, and I'd try to imagine such a tall building, my mind struggling to comprehend a structure that seemed to touch the clouds.

As I grew older, my curiosity about my grandmother and her life in Sarajevo grew. Why had she left? What was life like in the big city? These questions swirled in my mind, fueling a fascination with the world beyond our village.

Grandmother Zilka's visits from Sarajevo always brought a taste of city life to our rural village. Her arrival was marked by flavors that seemed exotic and exciting to my young palate. I remember the thrill of trying canned chicken spread for the first time - a delicacy that was a far cry from our usual homegrown fare. There was also salami, a treat we rarely had in our village, its rich, savory taste was a novelty that I savored. These city foods, along with other urban delicacies she'd bring, were like edible souvenirs from another world. Each bite was an adventure, a small taste of life beyond our village boundaries. These culinary experiences, simple as they might seem, opened my eyes to the diversity of tastes and experiences that existed beyond Žepa, fueling my curiosity about the wider world.

"One day, Adis, you'll visit Sarajevo," my father would say, noticing my wide-eyed fascination with Zilka's stories. "You'll see for yourself how different life can be."

These visits, and the story of my grandparents' divorce, planted seeds of curiosity in me about relationships, about the choices people make, and about the vast differences that can exist even within one country. I began to understand that the world was much larger and more complex than our small village, that people could choose different paths in life, even if those choices were difficult or unconventional.

As I grew older, this curiosity extended beyond just my family story. I became interested in the broader world, in the different ways people lived and the choices they made. The divorce, which had once seemed like a scandal, became in my mind a symbol of the complexity of human relationships and the courage it sometimes takes to forge one's own path.

This early exposure to a different way of life, through the story of my grandparents and Zilka's visits, played a significant role in shaping my worldview. It nurtured in me a desire to explore, to understand different perspectives, and to never judge a situation at face value. Little did I know then how crucial this openness to different ways of life would be in my future, as I navigated the challenges that lay ahead and eventually made my own journey to a new land.

A Special Day in Denim and Leather

There are some childhood memories that stand out vividly, painted in bright colors and rich with emotion. One such memory for me is of a particular day when our family visited my aunt Raza's village for the opening of a new mosque. It was a day of excitement, new experiences, and a special outfit that made me feel grown-up and important.

"Adis," my mother called early that morning, "come here. I have something special for you to wear today."

As I approached, my eyes widened with delight. There, laid out on the bed, was a complete denim outfit - a pair of jeans, a denim jacket, and even a small denim hat. It was the most fashionable thing I had ever seen, at least in my young eyes.

"Wow!" I exclaimed, running my hands over the sturdy fabric. "Is this really for me?"

Celebrating a special day in denim and leather, despite a little mishap with a bubble gum wrapper! Pictured here is my father, second from the right, and my uncle with his arm around me. The older man here was a dear friend of my father's.

My mother nodded, a warm smile on her face. "Yes, it's for you. Today is a special day, and you should look your best."

As she helped me into the outfit, I could hardly contain my excitement. I felt like a little man, dressed up just like the adults. The denim was stiff and new, rustling with every move I made.

But the outfit wasn't complete yet. There was one more surprise waiting for me at my aunt's house - a leather belt made by my uncle who worked in a leather shop.

As we arrived at Aunt Raza's village, the air was filled with the delicious aroma of roasted meats and the buzz of excitement for the mosque opening. But my mind was focused on one thing - finding my uncle.

"Where's Uncle?" I asked, tugging at my mother's sleeve. "Is he here?"

"Patience, Adis," she said with a laugh. "He'll be here soon."

And indeed, before long, I spotted him. "Uncle!" I called out, running towards him. "Do you have it?"

With a twinkle in his eye, he reached into his bag and pulled out a small leather belt, perfectly sized for a young boy. "Here you go, Adis," he said, handing it to me. "I made this especially for you."

I took the belt reverently, admiring the smooth leather and the shiny buckle. With help from my mother, I threaded it through the loops of my new jeans, completing my grown-up ensemble.

Proudly, I strutted around the gathering, my chest puffed out, feeling like the most stylish boy in all of Bosnia. The day was filled with joy - the solemn ceremony of the mosque opening, the feast that followed, and the excitement of the vendors selling their wares.

As the day wore on, I found myself drawn to a stand selling colorful gum. The long strips of gum, each piece wrapped individually in foil, caught my eye. Unable to resist, I bought a strip with the money my father had given me.

In my eagerness to try the gum, I wasn't as careful as I should have been. The sharp edge of the foil wrapper caught my finger, leaving a small cut. Not wanting to spoil the perfect day or dirty my new outfit, I tried to hide the injury, holding my hand carefully to prevent any blood from staining my clothes.

But mothers have a way of knowing these things. Before long, my mother noticed my discomfort and discovered the cut. As she tended to my finger, wrapping it carefully, I felt a mix of emotions - embarrassment at my clumsiness, but also warmth at her gentle care.

As the sun began to set and we prepared to leave, someone suggested taking a photograph to commemorate the day. I remember standing there, my bandaged finger hidden behind my back, my face a mixture of pride in my outfit and lingering embarrassment over my small mishap.

That photograph, capturing a young boy in a denim outfit with a prized leather belt, his finger secretly bandaged, became a cherished memento. It encapsulated so much of my childhood - the excitement of special occasions, the pride in new things, the small mishaps that seemed so big at the time, and the constant, comforting presence of family.

Looking back now, I smile at the memory of that day. The denim outfit and leather belt were more than just clothes - they were symbols of growing up, of being part of something bigger. They represented the love of family, the skills passed down through generations, and the simple joys that made life in our small Bosnian village so rich and meaningful.

The Gift of Ten Dinars

As we prepared to explore the festival-like atmosphere surrounding the mosque opening, my father reached into his pocket and pulled out something that made my eyes widen with excitement - a crisp, red 10-dinar note.

"Here, Adis," he said, his eyes twinkling as he placed the money in my small hand. "This is for you to spend as you wish today."

I held the banknote with reverence, marveling at its vibrant red color and the intricate designs that covered its surface. This wasn't just money; it was a work of art, a piece of our nation's identity held in my palm.

The note featured bold, patriotic motifs that captured the spirit of Yugoslavia. On one side, there was an image of a coal miner, his strong, muscular form representing the backbone of our country's industrial strength. The miner's determined expression seemed to embody the resilience and hard work of all Yugoslavs.

Beside the miner, I could see the iconic hammer and sickle, symbols of the communist ideology that shaped our nation. These emblems, far from being mere political markers to my young eyes, represented the unity and shared purpose of our diverse country.

On the other side of the note, the stern, commanding face of Marshal Tito gazed out. As our country's leader and a national hero, his image on the currency was a constant reminder of his role in shaping modern Yugoslavia.

The banknote felt special in my hands, almost too beautiful to spend. Its creases were crisp, suggesting it was newly minted, adding to my reluctance to part with it.

"Go on," my father encouraged, noticing my hesitation. "You can buy something nice with that."

As I clutched the red 10 dinar note, I felt a surge of responsibility. This wasn't just money; it was a symbol of trust from my father, a small step towards growing up. I knew I wanted to make a good choice with my purchase, to show my father that I could be trusted with this responsibility.

Little did I know then that this simple act of being given money to spend, this vibrant red banknote with its powerful imagery, was teaching me about more than just the value of currency. It was a lesson in our nation's values, in the trust between a father and son, and in the joy of making one's own choices. That 10 dinar note, with its red color and patriotic designs, became etched in my memory, a tangible link to a time and place that would soon change forever.

Reflecting Back

These memories, woven into the fabric of my childhood, remind me of the strength and resilience that shaped my life. From my mother's unwavering support to the playful adventures with my sisters, each moment was a thread in the tapestry of my early years—a story that continues to guide me, rooted in the land of Bosnia, a land of water, beauty, and enduring spirit.

As I reflect on those formative years, I am grateful for the love and lessons that surrounded me. They are the foundation upon which I stand, a constant reminder of where I come from and the strength that resides within me. The beauty of Bosnia, the warmth of family, and the resilience of my people are etched in my heart, a legacy I carry forward as I navigate the journey of life.

CHAPTER 2

Shadows of Change

As I entered second grade in 1990, the world around me began to change in subtle but significant ways. While our daily routines remained largely the same, there was an undercurrent of tension that even we children could sense. The carefree days of my early childhood were slowly giving way to a new reality, one that I couldn't fully comprehend at the time.

Our teacher, Miss Rosa Lazarević, continued to guide us through our lessons with the same dedication and care as always. An Orthodox Christian in our predominantly Muslim village, she embodied the spirit of Yugoslav unity that was increasingly under strain. Miss Rosa was a constant in our lives, her strict demeanor hiding genuine care for her students. Her classroom, with its pristine green desktops unmarred by a single scratch, was a haven of order and learning amidst the growing chaos outside.

Despite the growing tensions, Miss Rosa never brought politics into the classroom. She focused instead on teaching us to be good citizens and neighbors, emphasizing the values of hard work, respect, and community that had long been the bedrock of our society. Her lessons went beyond textbooks; she taught us practical skills like how to shop at the local grocery store, how to count change, and the importance of saying "please" and "thank you." These simple lessons in civility and responsibility would prove invaluable in the turbulent times ahead.

Outside the classroom, however, whispers of political unrest and growing tensions between the republics of Yugoslavia became more frequent. I remember coming home from school to find groups of adults huddled around television sets, their faces tight with concern as they watched the news. The air was thick with worry, though as children, we couldn't fully grasp its significance. Our parents tried to shield us from the worst of it, but we could sense their anxiety, like a heavy blanket settling over our once-peaceful village.

One day stands out clearly in my memory, a day that marked the beginning of the end of my childhood innocence. I had finished a test early and was allowed to leave school five minutes before the others - a small victory that filled me with excitement. As I ran down the hill from the school, relishing my head start on the long walk home through the forest, I was surprised to see my father waiting at the bottom.

"Adis," he called, his face serious. "Come with me."

The sight of my father there, instead of at work, sent a shiver of unease through me. Something was wrong, though I couldn't have guessed how wrong at the time.

He led me to the village water fountain where a crowd had gathered. There was an ambulance nearby, and the air was thick with tension. My father bought me some sweets, perhaps to distract me, as he explained that there had been fighting in Slovenia and Croatia. A local soldier, serving in the

Yugoslav People's Army, had been killed in the conflict, and his body was being returned to the village.

As we walked home through the forest, my father tried to reassure me. "There's nothing for us to worry about," he said, his voice steady but his eyes betraying his concern. "The Yugoslav People's Army will protect us. We are all brothers, after all."

But his words couldn't dispel the growing sense of unease. The forest path, once a place of adventure and mystery, now seemed fraught with unseen dangers. Every rustle in the leaves, every snapping twig, made me jump. The trees that had once seemed friendly giants now loomed ominously, their shadows deeper and more menacing than before.

In the weeks that followed, the situation deteriorated rapidly. The adults in the village spoke in hushed tones, their conversations stopping abruptly when children approached. The atmosphere in our home changed too. My parents spent long hours listening to the radio, their faces growing more worried with each passing day.

One day, Miss Rosa entered the classroom with a grave expression that silenced us all immediately. "Children," she said, her voice heavy with emotion, "the local villages are being attacked. It's not safe for us to continue school. We don't know when we'll be able to return."

As we left the school that day, there was a mix of excitement at the unexpected holiday and fear of the unknown. Walking home with my classmates, we speculated about what was happening, our young minds unable to grasp the full gravity of the situation. Some of us thought it might be an extended vacation, while others, picking up on the adults' anxiety, were more subdued.

The seriousness of the situation only hit me later when we arrived at home. I heard my parents speaking in hushed tones about the first casualties of the war. One name, the first - Suada Dilberović, killed by a sniper while she was on a bridge in Sarajevo. Her name was now immortalized on that same bridge, as that was where the war truly began.

As the days passed, the village changed. Men gathered whatever weapons they could find - hunting rifles, old pistols - and began to organize patrols in the hills around Žepa. The sense of community grew stronger even as the threat loomed larger. Neighbors who had once merely nodded in greeting now stopped to talk, to offer support, to share what little news they had. We were on our own now, cut off from the outside world as communication lines were severed and power outages became frequent.

The sudden isolation was jarring. The television, once a window to the wider world, now sat dark and silent in the corner of our living room. The postal service, which had brought letters and packages from relatives in distant cities, ceased to function. We were cut off, an island in a sea of uncertainty.

In those early days of the conflict, life took on a surreal quality. The routines of daily life continued - we still needed to eat, to wash, to sleep - but everything was tinged with an edge of fear. The sound of distant explosions became a regular occurrence, each boom making us wonder if we would be next.

A Winter Wedding: The Last Celebration Before the Storm

In December 1990, our village of Žepa was blanketed in snow, the pristine white a fitting backdrop for what would be one of the last joyous celebrations before our world changed forever. My oldest sister, Zilka, was getting married at the tender age of 17. At seven years old, I couldn't fully grasp the significance of the event, but I knew it was special.

"Adis," my mother called early that morning, "come help us prepare. Your sister is getting married today!"

The house was a flurry of activity. Neighbors streamed in and out, bringing dishes of food and offering help. The air was filled with the aroma of traditional Bosnian delicacies and the excited chatter of women.

Zilka sat in her room, surrounded by female relatives who fussed over her hair and makeup. I caught a glimpse of her, looking both nervous and beautiful with her 1980s-style big hair and a white wedding outfit that was more like a warm, elegant suit than a traditional gown – a practical choice for the winter weather.

Outside, cars began to arrive, decorated with colorful handkerchiefs and flags. The sound of honking horns and celebratory gunshots filled the air. My cousin Enver pulled me aside, his eyes twinkling with mischief.

"Listen, Adis," he whispered, "when your brother-in-law gives you money, make sure it's German marks, not Yugoslav dinars."

I nodded, not fully understanding the implications of his advice, but feeling important to be included in this adult conversation.

Soon, it was time for Zilka to leave. As her younger brother, it was my role to walk her out. My heart swelled with pride as I took her arm, leading her to the waiting cars. Snow crunched under our feet, and I could feel Zilka trembling slightly, whether from cold or excitement, I couldn't tell.

Her soon-to-be husband, Sead, approached us, a broad smile on his face. He handed me a wad of money – German marks, I noted with satisfaction – and then surprised me with a handful of fireworks.

"For you, little brother," he said, ruffling my hair.

As Zilka got into the best car in the convoy, I lit the fireworks, watching in awe as they exploded against the grey winter sky, sending sprays of snow flying. The wedding party departed in a cacophony of honking horns and cheers, leaving our yard suddenly quiet.

I found my younger sister, Mubera, standing alone, tears in her eyes. At 12 years old, she was caught between childhood and adolescence, and I could see the conflicting emotions on her face – joy for Zilka, but sadness at the change in our family.

"Want to play our secret language game?" I asked, trying to cheer her up. She nodded, and we spent the rest of the day inventing nonsense words, giggling in our own private world.

The next day at school, my teacher, Miss Rosa, commented on the wedding. "It was a lovely celebration," she said, her eyes twinkling. "But don't you think your sister is a bit young to be married? She should continue her education."

I felt a surge of pride that my family's customary wedding had been noticed and admired, even as I pondered Miss Rosa's words about education.

Looking back now, I realize that Zilka's wedding marked the end of an era. It was one of the last times our community came together in unbridled joy before the shadows of war began to loom. My sister, barely more than a child herself, was stepping into adulthood just as our world was about to be turned upside down.

Little did we know that in less than two years, Zilka would be back in Žepa, expecting her first child, fleeing the violence that had erupted in her new home of Rogatica. The winter wonderland of her wedding day would give way to the harsh realities of war, and the hopes and dreams we celebrated that day would be put on hold for years to come.

But on that snowy December day in 1990, all we knew was love, family, and celebration. It was a moment of pure joy, frozen in time like the icicles hanging from our roof – beautiful, fragile, and destined to melt away all too soon.

***

The carefree days of my early childhood were now firmly behind me. The lessons of unity and brotherhood that we had learned as Pioneers were being put to the test, and I was about to learn some much harder lessons about the world and my place in it.

As the conflict intensified, our village began to change in more visible ways. Gardens that had once grown flowers now sprouted vegetables, and every available patch of soil turned to the task of growing food. The playgrounds fell silent as parents kept their children close to home, the swings swaying emptily in the breeze.

Despite the growing danger, there were moments of beauty and resilience that stood out in my memory. I recall the day when old Habiba, known for her intricate embroidery, gathered the village children to teach us how to make traditional weaving baskets Krosnja for harvesting fruit, made from willow wood. "We must all do our part," she said, her gnarled hands guiding ours as we worked. "And we must not forget to live, even in these dark times."

It was in these moments - learning new skills, helping our neighbors, coming together as a community - that I began to understand the true strength of our people. We were more than just victims of a conflict we didn't understand; we were survivors, adapting and persevering in the face of unimaginable challenges.

As summer turned to autumn, and autumn to a bitter winter, the reality of our situation became impossible to ignore. The war, which had once seemed a distant threat, was now at our doorstep. The sounds of gunfire and explosions grew closer with each passing day.

Yet even in these darkest times, there were glimmers of hope. Miss Rosa, our teacher, refused to abandon her students. Though formal schooling had ceased, she began holding small classes in her home, teaching us by candlelight. "Knowledge," she would say, her eyes fierce with determination, "is something they can never take from you."

The world was changing, and with it, so was I. The innocent child who had once run laughing through sun-dappled forests was growing up far too quickly, forced to confront realities no child should face. Yet even as the shadows lengthened and the dangers grew, I held onto the lessons of my early childhood - the importance of community, the strength found in unity, and the power of hope in the face of adversity.

As we huddled together through those long, uncertain days, I realized that this too was a kind of education. We were learning not just how to survive, but how to hold onto our humanity in the darkest of times. It was a harsh lesson, but one that would shape the person I would become.

The Gathering Storm: Bosnia in the Brink

From 1990 to 1992, life in Bosnia began to change in ways I couldn't fully comprehend at the time. For most of us in Žepa, there was still a strong belief in the principles of old Yugoslavia. We clung to the idea that nothing catastrophic could happen, that we were all Yugoslavs, united under one flag.

Sarajevo, our capital, had long been considered the "Jerusalem of Europe," a place where different cultures and religions coexist peacefully. We believed this harmony would protect us from the growing tensions. I remember my parents often speaking about the multicultural nature of our country with pride, telling us children how lucky we were to grow up in such a diverse and tolerant society.

However, signs of trouble were becoming impossible to ignore. In the villages surrounding Žepa, predominantly populated by Orthodox Christians, people began hoarding supplies and emptying small grocery stores. Our parents, noticing this trend, started to do the same. They bought excess flour, sugar, salt, and oil – essentials that were usually only stockpiled in the fall to prepare for winter.

As a child of nine, I found this behavior curious. It was out of the ordinary, a disruption to the rhythms of life I had come to expect. I remember asking my mother why we needed so much flour when it wasn't even close to winter. She just smiled sadly and said, "It's always good to be prepared, Adis." Little did I know that these small changes were the first tremors of an approaching earthquake that would shatter our world.

The atmosphere in our village began to change. Conversations between adults would stop abruptly when children approached. The carefree laughter that once filled our streets became less frequent, replaced by hushed discussions and worried glances.

In Bosnia, President Alija Izetbegović tried to reassure the populace that everything would be fine. We would gather around our small television set, watching his speeches with a mixture of hope and growing unease. However, the actions and words of Serbian nationalists told a different story.

I remember a famous speech by Radovan Karadžić, a Bosnian Serb leader, in the Bosnian parliament. Even as a child, I could sense the tension in the room as he spoke. In a video that would become infamous, he openly declared that if Bosnia sought independence, it would not end well for Bosnian Muslims – that they would "disappear." The words sent a chill down my spine, even though I didn't fully understand their implications at the time.

President Izetbegović responded defiantly, assuring that Bosnian Muslims would not vanish and that if war came, they would defend themselves. I remember my father nodding grimly at the television, muttering, "It's coming. We must be ready."

This exchange marked a turning point. Soon after, barricades began appearing in the streets of Sarajevo and other cities. We heard news of the Serbian army ordering Serb civilians to evacuate from multicultural areas, particularly in Sarajevo. Later, we learned this was to ensure no Serbian civilians would be killed when they began shelling the city.

It's crucial to note that no one forced the Serbs to leave – many chose to stay. Even until 1995-1996, Bosnian Muslims only made up about 70% of the population in these areas. Our Serbian neighbors, people we had lived alongside peacefully for generations, were suddenly faced with an impossible choice – stay and risk being seen as traitors by their own people, or leave and abandon their homes and friends.

As 1992 progressed, the situation deteriorated rapidly. Electricity was cut off in many areas, severing our connection to the outside world. Our television, once a window to the wider world, now sat dark and silent in the corner of our living room. Small cities like Žepa, Srebrenica, and Zvornik in eastern Bosnia, near the Serbian border, lost contact with the capital.

I remember the day the electricity went out for good. We sat in the darkness, the flickering light of candles casting long shadows on the walls. My mother's face, illuminated by the soft glow, looked older somehow, worry etched into every line. That night, as I lay in bed listening to the unfamiliar silence of a village without power, I realized that the world I had known was gone forever.

I vividly remember my aunt Raza arriving – the same aunt we had visited for the opening of a new mosque just months before. Now she came as a refugee, her face gaunt with exhaustion and fear, bringing only what she could carry. Some arrived with livestock, desperate to save whatever they could of their livelihoods.

This picture shows Serbian Army soldiers with tanks targeting Zepa during the aggression.

Our once-quiet village transformed into a sanctuary, but our resources were stretched to the breaking point. People lived in basements, attics, sheds, and hastily constructed tents or log cabins. As winter approached, the situation became dire.

I remember helping my father and uncles build makeshift shelters, my small hands struggling with tools meant for adult use. The sound of hammering and sawing became a constant backdrop to our days, a rhythmic reminder of our desperate situation.

By mid-1992, we could see with our own eyes the buildup of enemy forces around us. Tanks and troops were visible on the horizon. I remember standing with my father on a hill overlooking the village, watching the distant movement of vehicles and men. "Remember this, Adis," he said, his voice tight with emotion. "This is what happens when people forget how to live together."

A critical moment came when we learned of a Serbian force of 150-200 troops with tanks advancing towards Žep, a nearby strategic location with a state-of-the-art military base built into a mountain. We knew that if they captured this base, it would be the end for us and for much of Eastern Bosnia.

The men of Žepa, including my father and uncles, gathered to mount a defense. They chose a canyon where a creek forms the beginnings of the Žepa River, with forests on both sides providing cover. I remember the night before they left, the somber atmosphere in our home as my mother packed what little food we could spare for my father. The look they exchanged as he walked out the door is etched in my memory – a mixture of love, fear, and determination.

Our defenders were poorly equipped, mostly carrying hunting rifles, with a few weapons brought by soldiers who had deserted from the fronts in Croatia or Slovenia. But what they lacked in firepower, they made up for in determination and ingenuity.

As the Serbian forces approached, our men felled huge logs across the road, creating obstacles for the tanks. When the tanks tried to climb over these logs, they would slide into ditches. The battle that ensued was fierce. My father later described it as a "rain of bullets" – so intense that it seemed impossible to avoid being hit.

We children were kept away from the fighting, but we could hear the distant sound of gunfire and explosions. The wait was agonizing. Would our fathers, uncles, and brothers return? Or would we be left defenseless against the advancing enemy?

Despite being outgunned, our defenders managed to repel the attack. More than half of the Serbian soldiers lost their lives, and only about 30 survived to be captured. When the news of victory reached us, there was a moment of jubilation. We had stood our ground against a superior force and prevailed. But the joy was short-lived, tempered by the knowledge that this was just the beginning of our struggle.

The aftermath of the battle revealed the complex nature of the conflict. The captured Serbian soldiers were initially held in an empty school in a nearby village. However, overnight, other Serbian forces attacked the village, killing some of their own captured soldiers in the process. The survivors were eventually exchanged for the bodies of Bosnian Muslims who had been killed. This grim trade – the living for the dead – became a recurring theme of the war.

I remember one such return vividly. My father, gaunt and exhausted, his clothes torn and muddy, appeared at our door after being gone for over a week. The look of relief on my mother's face as she embraced him is something I'll never forget. That night, we had a feast of sorts – a loaf of real bread and a jar of jam he had managed to trade for my mother's wedding ring.

This precious food was the result of a dangerous journey my father had undertaken. In those desperate times, men from Žepa would travel to Srebrenica, another UN-protected enclave, to exchange valuables for food. It was our only source of "trade" without money, a lifeline in a world where currency had lost its meaning. The risks were enormous, but so was the reward – a chance to feed their families, to see the relief in their children's eyes as they bit into real bread after weeks of deprivation.

As I watched my parents that night, I began to understand the true cost of our survival. Every morsel on our table was bought with sacrifice, every bite a testament to the lengths my parents would go to keep us alive. The trade of my mother's wedding ring for food was just one chapter in the ongoing story of our struggle, a story that connected us to countless other families fighting the same battle across the enclaves.

In that moment, the simple act of sharing bread and jam became something sacred, a communion of love and sacrifice that bound us together more strongly than any wedding ring ever could.

***

Spring and summer brought a bittersweet respite. The abundance of fruits, vegetables, and wild berries provided much-needed nourishment and a sense of normalcy. Seeing roses bloom and trees bud was a powerful reminder of life's persistence in the face of destruction. I would spend hours foraging in the woods with other children, our small hands stained with berry juice, momentarily forgetting the war that raged around us.

However, even these peaceful moments were often shattered by the sound of planes overhead, dropping bombs or incendiary devices that set the forests ablaze. The contrast between the natural beauty around us and the man-made hell we were living through was stark and painful.

There were disturbing signs that the enemy was using unconventional warfare tactics. Soldiers in the forest reported hallucinations and disorientation, leading to speculation about the use of biological weapons. The river would sometimes change color, suggesting chemical contamination. These experiences added a layer of psychological terror to the physical dangers we faced daily.

Throughout this period, the human cost of the war became increasingly clear. My sister Zilka, who had married in 1990 in the town of Rogatica, was forced to flee back to Žepa in late 1991. She arrived pregnant, giving birth to my niece in May 1992 amidst the chaos of war.

The contrast between her wedding – a joyous occasion full of hope for the future – and the reality she now faced was heartbreaking. Her husband, barely 20 years old, would leave for the front lines, and she never knew if he would return. The life they had dreamed of together was put on indefinite hold.

I remember watching my sister cradle her newborn daughter, tears streaming down her face as distant explosions punctuated the night. In that moment, I understood the true cruelty of war – not just in its physical destruction, but in its theft of dreams and futures.

A Brutal Awakening

The brutality of war spared no one, not even the animals that sustained our livelihoods. One summer day, as the conflict intensified, I experienced firsthand the devastating power of the shelling that had become a terrifying part of our daily lives.

Our house stood next to my uncle Emin's, where he kept a herd of sheep in his yard. On this particular day, the bombardment was relentless. We had always been told to seek shelter wherever we were when the shelling started, rather than risk running to a different location.

I found myself in our basement, curiosity overwhelming my fear. Despite the danger, I cracked open the door slightly, eager to see and hear what was happening outside. The familiar sequence began: the distant "doo, doo, doo" of artillery fire, followed by seconds of tense silence, then the ominous whistling of incoming shells.

At first, I thought they would pass overhead, but the sound grew closer and closer. Suddenly, a massive explosion rocked the earth, and everything went black.

When I regained consciousness, I found myself in a world of dust and debris. The basement windows were shattered, and I was lying atop my father's sharp tools - axes and saws from his days working in the lumber industry. As I struggled to my feet, pain shot through my body, and I felt warm blood where I had landed on the tools.

Dazed and disoriented, I made my way to the door. The sight that greeted me was one of utter devastation. My uncle's yard was a gruesome scene - his entire herd of sheep lay dead, their bodies torn apart by the blast. Pieces of flesh were scattered everywhere, a brutal testament to the destructive power of modern warfare.

Through the settling dust, I saw my uncle walking down the steep hill toward his yard, his face a mask of shock and disbelief. In a matter of seconds, his livelihood had been obliterated.

My senses were dulled from the explosion. Sounds seemed distant and muffled as if I were underwater. I could barely hear my mother's frantic calls, only becoming aware of her presence when I felt her hands on me, checking for injuries.

Our house hadn't escaped unscathed either. Chunks of the walls were missing, and shrapnel was embedded deep in the structure. It was a stark reminder of how close we had come to death.

This incident, etched forever in my memory, occurred sometime in 1993 before my uncle's passing. It was one of my closest encounters with death during the siege, a preview of the horrors we would face in our final journey from Žepa to free territory.

As I stood there, watching my uncle survey the remains of his flock, I was struck by the senseless destruction. The war hadn't just stolen our peace and our futures; it had obliterated our present, leaving nothing untouched in its wake. In that moment, covered in dust and blood, I felt a part of my childhood slip away, replaced by a grim understanding of the world we now inhabited.

Little did I know then how deeply these experiences would embed themselves in my psyche, resurfacing years later when I least expected it.

On December 31, 2019, nearly 25 years after leaving Bosnia, I found myself in Myrtle Beach, South Carolina, celebrating New Year's Eve with friends. As midnight approached and fireworks began to light up the sky, I was suddenly transported back to those terrifying days in Žepa.

The loud explosions, the bright flashes of light – they were no longer celebratory fireworks but the grenades and gunfire of my childhood. I froze, overwhelmed by emotions I thought I had long since buried. Tears streamed down my face as the memories flooded back, vivid and terrifying.

My friends, concerned and confused, tried to comfort me, but I was lost in the grip of a PTSD episode I didn't even know I had. It was the first time since coming to America that I had experienced such an intense reaction.

As I stood there on the beach, a grown man weeping at fireworks, I realized that the scars of war run deeper than I had ever imagined. The frightened boy from Žepa was still within me, still flinching at loud noises, still expecting danger from the sky.

In the days that followed, as I processed what had happened, I began to understand the true, lasting impact of what we had endured. The brutal awakening I experienced as a child in Žepa had shaped me in ways I was only now beginning to comprehend.

This realization brought with it a renewed appreciation for the strength and resilience of my family and community. We had survived not just the physical dangers of war, but the psychological trauma as well. And while the echoes of that trauma might never fully fade, understanding it became another step in my ongoing journey of healing.

As I reflect on both that morning in Žepa and that New Year's Eve in South Carolina, I am reminded of the enduring nature of human resilience. We carry our past with us always, but we also carry the strength that allowed us to survive it. In acknowledging both the pain and the perseverance, we honor our journey and continue to move forward, one day at a time.

A New Life Amidst Chaos

In the midst of war's darkness, a single moment of pure joy illuminated our lives. It was May 1992, just as a major battle raged and the Serbian army faced defeat near our village. But within the walls of our family home, a different kind of struggle was taking place—one that would bring new life into our war-torn world.

I was just nine years old, perched anxiously on the edge of our living room sofa. The air was thick with tension, but it was different from the fear we'd grown accustomed to. My mother darted between rooms, her face a mask of concentration. My brother-in-law, Sead, mirrored her movements, his usual calm demeanor replaced by nervous energy.

I knew my sister Zilka was pregnant, but in my childish understanding, I hadn't fully grasped what that meant. Now, as I watched the adults' urgent activity, I sensed that something monumental was happening.

Suddenly, piercing through the muffled sounds of distant shelling, came a new sound—the unmistakable cry of a baby. My heart leaped. "What just happened?" I wondered, my eyes wide with surprise.

Moments later, Sead emerged from the bedroom, his face pale and stunned, as if he'd witnessed a miracle. Which, I suppose, he had. My mother followed, her voice filled with a joy I hadn't heard in months as she announced, "It's a girl!"

I watched in awe as my mother, this pillar of strength who had delivered me years ago, gently carried out a tiny bundle wrapped in clean linens. She placed the baby in my sister's arms, and I marveled at the sight. Zilka, exhausted but radiant, cradled her newborn daughter with a look of fierce love and protection.

Our home, which had felt increasingly oppressive under the weight of war, suddenly buzzed with new energy. Family members and neighbors crowded around, eager to catch a glimpse of this miracle—a new life defiantly entering our world even as death loomed all around us.

Later that day, I witnessed another first. The local imam arrived to recite the Adhan, the Islamic call to prayer, in the baby's ear. Fascinated, I tugged at my mother's sleeve. "Why is he doing that?" I whispered.

She smiled down at me, her eyes soft. "It's so the first words the child hears are a reminder of Allah," she explained. "It's a blessing and a welcome."

As I watched this centuries-old tradition unfold, I felt a connection to something greater than myself, greater even than the war that had consumed our lives. I thought about my own birth, wondering who had recited the Adhan for me. It was a man long gone now, but the thought created a bridge between past and present, just as this tiny baby formed a bridge to our future.

In that moment, as I gazed at my newborn niece, I felt a surge of protectiveness. I was an uncle now, even if I was more like a brother in age. Little did I know then how profound that relationship would become.

Years later, in the United States, our bond deepened further. For three years, while her parents were still trying to join us, my niece lived with me in a tiny studio apartment. I was in my twenties, juggling work and college, and suddenly responsible for this young life. Our days were a whirlwind—me waking at 4 a.m. for work, rushing to classes, studying whenever I could, and ferrying her between home and her own job.

It was exhausting, often overwhelming, but it forged a connection between us that was unbreakable. In many ways, I became a parent before I was ready, guiding and protecting her as we navigated our new life in America.

Now, looking back on that day in May 1992, I see it as a turning point. In the darkest days of the war, when hope seemed lost, the birth of my niece, Selma reminded us all of life's persistence. She was our family's small act of defiance against the destruction around us, a promise that no matter what happened, life would go on.

That day, in our little house in Žepa, as bombs fell and battles raged, we celebrated new life. We dared to hope for a future, even as our present crumbled around us. And in that hope; in that tiny, wailing bundle, we found the strength to carry on.

Symbol of Lost Innocence

It was only later, at home, that I began to understand the seriousness of our situation. My parents again spoke in hushed tones. They mentioned a name that would forever be etched in the history of our conflict - Suada Dilberović.

"Who was she?" I asked, curiosity overcoming my fear to ask about who they were talking about.

My father's face grew solemn. "Suada Dilberović," he said, his voice heavy with emotion, "was a young medical student from Dubrovnik. She was only 24 years old, Adis. Just a few years older than your sisters."

He went on to explain that on April 5, 1992, Suada had joined thousands of other peace demonstrators on the Vrbanja Bridge in Sarajevo. They were protesting against the division of the city along ethnic lines. It was supposed to be a peaceful demonstration, a show of unity in the face of growing tensions.

"But then," my mother interjected, her eyes glistening with unshed tears, "Serbian snipers opened fire on the crowd. Suada was one of the first to fall."

I tried to imagine it - a bright, promising young woman, not much more than a girl really, cut down in the prime of her life. It seemed impossible, incomprehensible.

The death of Suada Dilberović, the first casualty of the war, marked the beginning of a new, terrifying era. Violence became commonplace. Any gathering or sign of resistance was met with shelling, grenades, or sniper fire. Small groups of Bosnian Serbs would terrorize Bosnian Muslim neighborhoods, killing and plundering.

In Žepa, we felt the impact of these events keenly. Communication became sparse, with news traveling slowly if at all. We began to see an influx of Bosnian Muslims from surrounding areas, including my cousins and other family members. The population of our small town quadrupled almost overnight.

"She wasn't the only one," my father continued. "Another young woman, Olga Sučić, was also killed that day. She was Catholic and Suada Muslim. They became the first victims of the Siege of Sarajevo, which would last for nearly four years. Just the first of Muslims, Catholics, and even Orthodox Christians to die by Serb Army hands. They did not spare anyone."

The weight of this knowledge pressed heavily on my young shoulders, grounding me in a reality I could barely comprehend. These were not just names in a news report or numbers in a history book—they were real people. People with dreams and aspirations, with families who cherished them. And now, they were gone, their lives violently cut short by a conflict they had tried so desperately to prevent.

As we stood in solemn silence, my father's voice broke through the stillness, low and heavy with emotion. "The bridge where they fell," he said, almost a whisper, "has been renamed in their honor. It's now called the Suada and Olga Bridge—a tribute to their sacrifice, a reminder of the cost of this war, and the bravery of those who dare to stand for peace." His words lingered in the air, the weight of their meaning sinking deeper into my heart.

That night, lying in bed, I couldn't shake the image of Suada Dilberović from my mind. She became more than just a name to me—she was a symbol, a poignant reminder of all that was at stake in this relentless conflict. Her story, steeped in tragedy, stirred something profound within me. Even as a child, I felt a burgeoning resolve, a need to remember her and others like her. I didn't fully understand what it meant to bear witness, but I knew, even then, that her story demanded to be carried forward.

The bridge that now bore her name became more than just a structure in a distant city. It became a symbol of the line we were all walking - between peace and war, between unity and division, between life and death. Suada's sacrifice, and that of countless others like her, would not be forgotten.

As the conflict intensified and more names were added to the growing list of casualties, I often found myself thinking of Suada. Her story became a touchstone for me, a reminder of the human cost of war and the importance of standing up for what's right, even in the face of danger.

Reflecting Back

The war robbed an entire generation of their youth and dreams. My sister, like so many others, never got the chance to live the life she had imagined. Married at 17, a mother at 18, and a refugee by 19, her story became a testament to the resilience of the human spirit in the face of unimaginable adversity.

Looking back on those years in Žepa, it's hard to convey the full scope of what we experienced. Every day brought new challenges, new losses, and new reasons to despair. Yet somehow, we found the strength to continue, to help each other, to hold onto our humanity in the face of unspeakable horror.

The siege of Žepa, like the larger Bosnian War, was a testament to both the depths of human cruelty and the heights of human resilience. We experienced loss on a scale that's difficult to comprehend – loss of lives, of homes, of innocence. But we also witnessed incredible acts of bravery, kindness, and selflessness.

I saw neighbors share their last scraps of food, risking their lives to help others escape, comforting each other in the darkest hours. I learned that even in the face of hatred and violence, love and compassion can survive.

As a child living through this nightmare, I was forced to grow up far too quickly. The carefree days of my early childhood were replaced by a constant struggle for survival. But amidst the hardship and horror, there were also invaluable lessons – about the strength of community, the importance of family, and the resilience of the human spirit.

These memories, painful as they are, are a part of who I am. They've shaped my worldview, my values, and my understanding of both the fragility of peace and the enduring strength of the human spirit. They drive me to share this story, not just as a record of what happened, but as a warning about the consequences of hatred and division, and a testament to the power of hope and unity in the darkest of times.

The storm that engulfed Žepa and all of Bosnia may have passed, but its effects linger. As I look at the world today, I see echoes of the same forces that tore my country apart. My hope is that by sharing these experiences, we can learn from history and work towards a world where such atrocities never happen again.

CHAPTER 3

The Long Winter

As the siege of Žepa continued, life took on a surreal quality. The year after the battle for Žepa stretched before us like an endless, harsh winter. Every day brought new challenges and tragedies. Grenades would fall, killing people and destroying homes. Each day blended into the next, marked only by the constant rhythm of explosions and the ever-present fear that gripped our hearts.

Illness became a constant threat, with no access to medical care. People died from treatable conditions like appendicitis, or from cold and flu in the harsh winter months. My uncle Emin, my father's brother, died in 1993 or 1994 from kidney complications. At only 38 years old, his slow, painful death was a stark reminder of our isolation and vulnerability. There was no way to get him the medical help he needed – no helicopters, no outside communication, no hope of rescue. I remember the helplessness in my father's eyes as he watched his brother slip away, unable to do anything to save him.

I remember waking up one morning to the sound of distant shelling. The sun had barely risen, casting long shadows across our small room. My mother was already up, her face etched with worry as she peered out the window.

"Adis," she whispered, motioning me over. "Come, but stay low."

I crept to her side, and together we watched as plumes of smoke rose from the eastern part of Žepa. The Serbs were retaliating for our successful defense of Žepa, their fury manifesting in a rain of grenades and sniper fire.

"Why won't they stop, Majka?" I asked, my voice small in the face of such relentless violence.

She pulled me close, her arms trembling slightly. "Because, my son, they cannot accept that we dare to exist, that we dare to defend ourselves."

A New Way of Life

As the days wore on, we adapted to this new reality. Working in the fields during daylight became too dangerous, so people shifted their activities to the evenings and nights. I'd watch as my father and the other men of the village slipped out after sunset, tools in hand, to tend to what crops they could under the cover of darkness.

One night, as my father prepared to leave, I tugged at his sleeve. "Can I come with you, Babo? I want to help."

He knelt down, his eyes level with mine. "Adis, I need you to stay here and protect your mother and sisters. Can you do that for me?"

I nodded solemnly, puffing out my chest with the importance of my assigned task. It was only years later that I understood he was protecting me, shielding me from the dangers that lurked in the darkness.

The River of Death

As the war intensified around 1993 and 1994, the horrors we faced took on new, unimaginable forms. The River Drina, once a symbol of natural beauty and the lifeblood of our region, became a grim messenger of terror.

One evening, I overheard my father talking in hushed tones with other men from our village. Their faces were ashen, their voices trembling with a mix of rage and despair.

"They're sending bodies down the river," my father said, his voice barely above a whisper. "From Višegrad. It's... it's inhuman."

I didn't fully understand then, but I knew something terrible was happening. Later, I learned the full extent of this horror. The Serbs in Višegrad, a town upstream on the Drina, had begun a campaign of psychological warfare that defied all bounds of human decency.

Fishermen in Žepa, who once cast their nets for sustenance, now found themselves retrieving corpses from the murky waters. The stories they brought back chilled us to the bone. Women were stripped of both clothes and dignity, tied to doors, and set adrift. Men bound to logs, their lifeless bodies a macabre flotilla of terror. Each gruesome discovery was a deliberate act, meant to break our spirit and crush our will to resist.

Though I never saw these nightmarish scenes myself, the descriptions seared themselves into my young mind. I imagined the river, which I had always seen as a source of life, now transformed into a conveyor belt of death.

The thought of it made me sick to my stomach.

"Why are they doing this, Babo?" I asked my father one night, unable to shake the images from my mind.

He pulled me close, his strong arms trembling slightly. "They want to scare us, Adis. They want us to give up. But we won't. We can't."

I learned that brave men from our community were working tirelessly to retrieve these bodies, determined to give them a proper burial despite the risk. A mass grave was established as a solemn testament to the cruelty we faced. Most of the victims remain unnamed, their identities lost to the river's cruel current, but not forgotten.

The River Drina, which had once flowed peacefully past our town, joining with the River Žepa to form a picturesque lake, now carried with it the weight of unspeakable crimes. It became a symbol of the war's brutality, a constant reminder of the forces arrayed against us.

Yet, even in the face of such horror, our community did not break. We mourned, we raged, we feared – but we did not surrender. The very act of retrieving those bodies, of laying them to rest with what dignity we could muster, was an act of defiance. It was a statement that even in our darkest hour, we would not abandon our humanity.

Even as we grappled with this psychological assault, life in Žepa struggled on. During brief lulls in the fighting, people ventured out to gather lumber, preparing shelters for the harsh winter ahead. I remember the hope in their eyes as they worked, the determination to survive despite everything.

But even this small comfort was short-lived. As we fled to the mountains in the final days of Žepa, I saw those same shelters engulfed in flames, the fruits of so much labor and hope reduced to ash and smoke. It was a sight that broke something inside me, a final cruel lesson in the ruthlessness of our enemies.

As a child, I struggled to comprehend the scale of this evil. How could anyone deliberately inflict such terror? How could they seek to destroy not just our bodies, but our very souls? It was a harsh awakening to the depths of human cruelty, one that would shape my understanding of the world for years to come.

As I reflect on these memories now, I am struck by the resilience of my people. In the face of calculated terror, designed to strip us of hope and dignity, we found the strength to carry on. We held onto our values, and our compassion, even as the world around us descended into madness. It was a powerful lesson in the indomitable nature of the human spirit, one that would sustain me through the trials yet to come.

The Influx of Refugees

The influx of refugees from surrounding areas strained our already meager resources. Familiar faces were outnumbered by strangers, each with their own harrowing tale of escape. Our small house became a sanctuary for distant relatives I had never met before.

One evening, as we huddled around a small fire for warmth, my aunt Raza, who had fled from a neighboring village, began to weep softly.

"What's wrong, tetka?" I asked, alarmed by her tears.

She tried to smile through her sorrow. "Nothing, Adis. I was just remembering my home, my garden. The roses would be blooming now."

My mother reached out and squeezed her hand. "One day, Raza, you'll plant new roses. We must hold onto hope."

The Dangers of Childhood

Hope, however, was in short supply. Even the simplest childhood pleasures became fraught with danger. One afternoon, while playing with my cousins, I fell and scraped my knee badly. In normal times, it would have been a minor incident, quickly treated and forgotten. But these were not normal times.

"Adis!" my mother exclaimed when she saw the blood. "Come here, let me look at that."

She cleaned the wound as best she could with our dwindling supply of clean water, her forehead creased with worry. "We must keep this clean," she muttered, more to herself than to me. "We can't risk an infection."

I nodded bravely, trying not to show how much it hurt. Infections had become a serious threat, with no antibiotics and limited medical supplies. I had seen adults succumb to what should have been treatable ailments. The memory of my uncle Emin's recent death from kidney complications was still fresh in everyone's minds.

The Arrival of Peacekeepers

It was in this atmosphere of constant danger and deprivation that we received news that offered a glimmer of hope. The United Nations had declared Žepa a safe zone and was sending peacekeepers.

"Peacekeepers?" I asked my father, the unfamiliar word rolling off my tongue. "What does that mean?"

He explained as best he could, though I could see uncertainty in his eyes. "They're soldiers, but they're not here to fight. They're here to protect us, to keep the peace."

When the peacekeepers finally arrived, it was like a scene from another world. A convoy of white vehicles with large UN letters rolled into town, driven by soldiers wearing blue helmets. The sight was so strange, so out of place in our war-torn village, that for a moment, we all stood in stunned silence.

Then, as if a spell had been broken, people began to cheer. Children ran alongside the vehicles, waving and shouting. For the first time in months, I saw genuine smiles on the faces of the adults.

Education Amidst Chaos

As the peacekeepers set up their base, taking over our school building, life in Žepa began to change once again. Classes were moved to makeshift locations - the postal service building, a converted textile factory, and even outdoors when the weather permitted.

I'll never forget the day we had our first outdoor lesson. We sat in rows on the grass outside the old textile factory, the sun was warm on our backs as our teacher, Miss Rosa, taught us multiplication tables. The sound of her voice, firm yet kind, was occasionally drowned out by the rumble of UN vehicles passing nearby.

"Now, who can tell me what seven times eight is?" Miss Rosa asked, her eyes scanning our eager faces.

Just as I was about to raise my hand, a loud explosion echoed in the distance. We all flinched, instinctively ducking our heads. Miss Rosa's face paled, but she quickly composed herself.

"It's alright, children," she said, her voice steady despite the fear I could see in her eyes. "We're safe here. Now, where were we? Ah yes, seven times eight."

Sparks of Ingenuity

Life continued in this surreal fashion. The presence of the peacekeepers brought a sense of security, but it didn't solve all our problems. Food was still scarce, and people resorted to extreme measures to feed their families.

One day, I found my mother in the kitchen, carefully opening a fire extinguisher. Confused, I asked her what she was doing.

"We need baking soda, Adis," she explained, her voice tight with concentration. "There's some inside these extinguishers. We have to use everything we can find."

I watched in amazement as she extracted the white powder, treating it like precious gold. Later that day, I saw her grinding dried apple peelings into a flour-like substance.

"What's that for, Majka?" I asked.

She managed a small smile. "We're going to make bread, my clever boy. It won't taste like what we're used to, but it will fill our stomachs."

In the midst of war's deprivations, we found ways to create light from darkness – both literally and figuratively. One day, while exploring the outskirts of our village, I stumbled upon a collection of abandoned Soviet trucks. They stood like rusted sentinels, relics of a bygone era. Most were stripped bare, but one caught my eye – it still had its battery.

Excitement bubbled up inside me as I raced home, my feet barely touching the ground. "SEAD!" I called out to my brother-in-law as I burst through the door. "I found a truck battery!"

Sead's eyes lit up with a spark I hadn't seen in months. "Show me," he said, already heading for the door.

Together, we made our way back to the truck. The battery was massive, far heavier than I had anticipated. At just nine years old, I could barely budge it. But Sead, in his late twenties and far stronger, managed to hoist it onto his shoulder. I watched in awe as he carried our precious cargo home, his face set with determination despite the obvious strain.

Back home, Sead set to work immediately. With deft hands, he connected wires to a small light bulb. We held our breath as he made the final connection. Suddenly, light flooded the room – a tiny sun in our war-darkened world. The joy on everyone's faces was indescribable. For the first time in years, we had driven back the darkness, if only in this small way.

But our victory was short-lived. The battery's charge wouldn't last forever, and we faced a new challenge: how to recharge it. Sead's resourcefulness shone through once again. His uncle had an old diesel truck, but fuel was scarce. Undeterred, they managed to procure some crude oil, just enough to get the engine running.

For the next few weeks, a strange ritual unfolded. Every few days, Sead and his uncle would drive the truck up and down our street, the engine's rumble a stark contrast to our usually quiet village. It was just enough to recharge our precious battery. This cycle of use and recharge became a part of our daily life, a small triumph of human ingenuity over the hardships of war.

As winter approached, our community's resourcefulness was tested further. With lumber in short supply, one man from a nearby village transformed an abandoned bus into a makeshift home. I remember watching in fascination as they gutted the interior, replacing seats with crude furniture and covering windows with plywood. It was a stark reminder of our desperate circumstances, yet also a testament to human adaptability.

That winter brought its own set of challenges and unexpected joys. Snow blanketed our village, piling up to four or five feet in places. For us children, it was a wonderland. We fashioned skis from old crates and spent hours sliding down the slopes, our laughter echoing through the crisp air.

I remember zooming past the converted bus house, marveling at the strange sight of smoke rising from a vehicle's roof. It was surreal, like something out of a fairy tale, yet it was our reality.

My mother, ever vigilant, would warn us about getting wet and falling ill. "Adis," she'd call out, her voice tinged with worry, "come inside before you catch your death!"

But the allure of play was too strong. We'd sneak out, reveling in our small acts of rebellion against the constraints of our situation. The exhilaration of sliding down the snow-covered slopes was worth any potential scolding.

Strangely, the heavy snowfall brought an unexpected respite. The thick blanket of snow muffled the sounds of distant shelling and explosions. It was as if nature itself was trying to shield us, if only for a moment, from the harsh realities of war.

Looking back, I'm struck by the contradictions of that time. Amidst the terror and hardship, we found moments of joy and triumph. We made light from abandoned batteries, homes from discarded vehicles, and playgrounds from war-torn landscapes. It was a harsh education in resilience and creativity, one that would shape us all in the years to come.

These memories – the warmth of that single light bulb, the absurdity of a bus-turned-house, the exhilaration of sliding down snowy slopes – are etched deeply in my mind. They serve as reminders that even in the darkest times, the human spirit finds ways to persevere, to create, and even to find joy. It was through these small acts of defiance against our circumstances that we maintained our humanity and hope for a better future.

The Struggle for Sustenance

As winter approached, new challenges arose. The few livestock that remained couldn't be slaughtered for meat because their milk was too precious, but feeding them was a constant struggle. I often accompanied my father and the other men as they ventured out at night to harvest hay, which they would then dry during the day to feed the animals.

One particularly cold night, as we worked quickly and quietly in a field on the outskirts of town, my father suddenly froze. He raised his hand, signaling for silence. Even though our village was far from the roads where the Serbs patrolled, in the distance, we could hear the low rumble of engines. These were planes flying over.

"Serb patrol," he whispered. "Everyone down, now!"

We dropped to the ground, our hearts pounding. I could feel the cold, damp earth against my face as I lay there, barely daring to breathe. The sound of the engines grew louder, then gradually faded away. Only when we could no longer hear them did my father signal that it was safe to move.

A Father's Promise

As we gathered our meager harvest and prepared to head back, I saw the toll this constant fear was taking on my father. In the pale moonlight, he looked older, his face lined with worry and exhaustion.

"Babo," I said softly, "are we going to be okay?"

He turned to me, and for a moment, I saw a flicker of the man he used to be - strong, confident, unafraid. He placed his hand on my shoulder and squeezed gently.

"We will survive this, Adis," he said, his voice low but firm. "We are Bosnians. We are strong. And we will never give up."

As we made our way back to the village, I clung to those words, repeating them in my mind like a mantra. We are Bosnians. We are strong. We will never give up.

The Diversity

The presence of the UN peacekeepers brought new experiences and challenges. The diversity of the peacekeeping force - Ukrainians, French, even some African troops - was a cultural shock in our small, homogeneous town.

One day, my curiosity overcame my shyness, and I approached a group of African peacekeepers. A translator stood nearby, looking slightly impatient, as if he should be tending to more serious matters than a little boy's questions during wartime.

"Where are you from?" I asked in Bosnian, my words relayed through the translator. At that time, I didn't speak English, and the only foreign language taught in our schools before the war was Russian.

One of the soldiers smiled kindly as he heard the translation. "We are from Ghana," he replied, his words then converted to Bosnian for me. "It's a country in Africa, very far from here."

I nodded, trying to imagine a place so distant, so different from my war-torn home. "Is it peaceful there?" I asked, the word 'peaceful' feeling strange on my tongue, almost forgotten.

The soldier's smile faltered for a moment as he heard my question. "It has its own challenges," he said diplomatically, his words once again filtered through the translator. "But nothing like what you're facing here. You're very brave, young man."

The translator, who previously looked uncomfortable amid the harshness of the war-torn area, now seemed to soften a bit as he relayed these words, perhaps realizing the importance of this small exchange.

His words stayed with me, making me wonder about the world beyond our borders, beyond this war. It was a small reminder that life existed outside of our daily struggle for survival and that even in the midst of chaos, human connection could bridge vast distances and differences.

Conflicted Peacekeepers

Despite the peacekeepers' presence, the threat of violence never truly disappeared. The Serbs would still occasionally shell remote areas where the UN forces weren't stationed. The Ukrainian peacekeepers' apparent sympathy for the Serbs - whom they considered 'brothers' due to their shared Orthodox faith - was a source of confusion and concern for many of us.

One day, I overheard two Ukrainian peacekeepers talking as they patrolled near our makeshift school.

"It's our brothers doing the shooting," one said to the other in Russian, not realizing I could understand some of what they were saying. "How can we be expected to fight against them?"

Their words sent a chill down my spine. If even our protectors saw our enemies as brothers, who could we truly rely on?

Whispers of Hope and Sacrifice

As the siege dragged on, moments of hope became increasingly rare and precious. In 1994, we began to hear rumors that the Bosnian forces were organizing more effectively, even managing to capture some helicopters and other weapons.

These rumors were confirmed one night when we were woken by the distant thrum of helicopter rotors. The sound filled me with a mixture of excitement and fear.

"Babo, what's happening?" I whispered, shaking my father awake.

He listened for a moment, then a slow smile spread across his face. "Those are our helicopters, Adis. They're bringing supplies."

We rushed outside, joining our neighbors as we watched the dark shapes of the helicopters pass overhead. It was a dangerous mission - we all knew the pilots risked being shot down - but it was also a lifeline, bringing much-needed supplies and a connection to the outside world.

Tragically, these missions didn't always succeed. One night, we heard a helicopter approaching, only for the sound to be suddenly cut off, followed by a distant explosion. The next day, word spread that the helicopter had crashed due to bad weather and enemy fire, killing all on board.

The loss was keenly felt by everyone. These brave pilots, risking their lives to bring us aid, had become symbols of hope. Their deaths were a harsh reminder of the price of our survival.

Learning Amidst the Chaos

Throughout these dark days, education remained a priority. When communication was reestablished with the Bosnian government through UNPROFOR, we received guidance on what to study. The arrival of notebooks and pencils as part of the aid was cause for excitement - something new in our deprived world.

"Look, Adis," my cousin Emir said one day, showing me his new notebook. "It's completely blank. No one has ever written in it before."

We marveled at the clean, crisp pages, running our fingers over the smooth paper. It was a small thing, but in those days, even the smallest luxuries felt miraculous.

Reflecting back

As I look back on those harrowing days in Žepa, the memories still have the power to overwhelm me. The siege that seemed endless, the constant struggle for survival, and the looming threat of violence shaped my childhood in ways I'm still understanding today.

The arrival of the UN peacekeepers, which seemed like salvation at the time, now feels bittersweet in retrospect. While they brought some measure of security and connection to the outside world, their presence also highlighted the complexities of international intervention. The conversation I had with the Ghanaian peacekeeper, which seemed so profound to my young self, now strikes me as a poignant reminder of how isolated we were, how little the outside world truly understood our plight.

Education, which remained a priority even in those dark times, proved to be our lifeline to normalcy and hope for the future. Miss Rosa's determination to continue teaching, even as explosions echoed in the distance, was an act of resistance against the chaos that threatened to engulf us. It taught me the value of knowledge and the power of maintaining routine in the face of adversity.

The loss of my uncle Emin to a treatable condition stands out as one of the war's cruelest ironies. In a world of violence, it was the lack of basic medical care that took him from us. His death underscores the often-overlooked casualties of war - those who fall not to bullets or bombs, but to the collapse of essential services we take for granted in peacetime.

As I share these stories with my nieces and nephews now, I'm struck by how surreal they must seem to them. The idea of scrounging for food, of living under constant threat, is as foreign to them as peace seemed to us then. Yet I feel compelled to pass on these memories, not to burden them, but to instill in them the values that saw us through: resilience, community, and hope.

The siege of Žepa robbed me of a carefree childhood, but it also gave me profound lessons in human strength and solidarity. It showed me that even in the darkest times, people can find ways to support each other, to maintain their dignity, and to hold onto hope. These are the lessons I carry with me, the silver lining I've found in the storm clouds of war. They are the legacy of Žepa, a testament to the unbreakable spirit of its people.

CHAPTER 4

The Crumbling Sanctuary

As 1994 dawned, the delicate peace we had known in Žepa began to crumble. The war across Bosnia had reached its zenith, with the Bosnian army making advances in central, southern, and northern territories. But our small enclave, along with Srebrenica, found itself under increasing pressure from the Serbian forces.

"Adis," my mother said one evening, her voice tight with worry, "the supplies are getting scarcer. We must be careful with what we have."

I nodded, understanding the gravity of her words. The convoys that once brought us food and hope were becoming less frequent. The Serbs were tightening their grip, slowly strangling our lifeline to the outside world.

The Hidden Dangers

One crisp autumn morning, as I walked to school along the familiar forest path, I noticed an unusual commotion near the town's makeshift hospital. Curiosity got the better of me, and I inched closer, my mother's constant warnings echoing in my ears.

"Adis," she would say, her eyes filled with worry, "stay close to the trees. Avoid open spaces. The mines don't discriminate between soldiers and children."

As I approached, the acrid smell of antiseptic mingled with the metallic scent of blood. An ambulance—really just a converted urgent care van—was parked outside. But it wasn't the vehicle that made my heart stop; it was what I saw next to it.

Sitting on makeshift benches were men—some soldiers, some civilians—all missing legs. Their empty pant legs fluttered in the breeze, a grim reminder of the hidden dangers that lurked in our once-peaceful fields and roads. Among them, to my horror, I recognized two faces: classmates of mine, barely older than my 12 years, now irrevocably changed by the cruel randomness of war.

"What happened?" I whispered to a nearby nurse.

She looked at me, her eyes heavy with fatigue and sorrow. "Landmines," she said simply. "They wandered into a minefield while playing."

I stood there, rooted to the spot, as the full weight of our reality crashed down upon me. These were kids I had laughed with, played with, shared dreams of the future with. Now, those futures had been violently altered in the blink of an eye.

As I finally turned to continue my journey to school, I found myself hyper-aware of every step. The forest path I had trodden a hundred times suddenly seemed fraught with invisible dangers. I hugged the treeline, just as my mother had taught me, my eyes scanning for any disturbed earth or suspicious objects.

That evening, as I recounted what I had seen to my mother, her face paled. She pulled me into a fierce hug, her body trembling slightly.

"Promise me, Adis." she whispered, her voice choked with emotion, "Promise me you'll always be careful. Stay with groups, and stick to known paths. I couldn't bear to lose you too."

I nodded solemnly, the image of my legless classmates burned into my memory. In that moment, I understood that in Žepa, even the ground beneath our feet could betray us. The war had not just changed our present; it had booby-trapped our future, leaving scars that would last long after the last bullet was fired.

Manna from the Sky

In these dire times, we found hope in the most unexpected places. One night, I was awakened by the distant hum of aircraft engines. My heart raced, torn between fear of bombing and hope for aid.

"Babo," I whispered, shaking my father awake, "do you hear that?"

He listened for a moment, then a slow smile spread across his face. "Those aren't bombers, Adis. They're bringing us supplies."

We rushed outside, joining our neighbors as we watched the dark shapes of planes pass overhead. Parachutes blossomed in the night sky, their payloads descending slowly to the earth. Phosphorus lights guided their way, creating an eerie, beautiful spectacle.

"Look, Adis," my cousin Emir exclaimed, pointing to the falling packages, "it's like magic!"

But this magic came with its own dangers. We heard stories of people killed by falling crates, crushed under the weight of the very aid meant to save them. Still, the promise of food and supplies was too tempting to ignore.

Necessity: The Mother of Invention

In the midst of our struggle for survival, an unexpected silver lining emerged from the aid parachutes that dotted our mountains. These lifelines, which brought us vital supplies, soon became a source of raw materials for our resourceful community.

I remember the day my mother first brought home a bundle of parachute fabric. Her eyes gleamed with possibility as she spread it out on our kitchen table. "Look, Adis," she said, running her hand over the material. "We can make something of this."

Soon, our home like many others in Žepa, became a hub of creative industry. Women gathered, their nimble fingers transforming the hodgepodge of fabrics – some cotton-like and pliable, others a tougher nylon – into clothing. The constant whir of hand-cranked sewing machines and the soft murmur of conversation became the soundtrack of our days.

But it wasn't just clothing. Our ingenuity knew no bounds. I watched in fascination as my neighbors breathed new life into discarded shoe soles, marrying them with parachute fabric to create sturdy footwear. Inspired, I decided to try my hand at this new craft.

"I want to make my own sandals," I announced one day, determination overriding my lack of experience.

My mother smiled, handing me a needle and some tough parachute material. "Be careful," she warned. "The needle is sharp."

She wasn't wrong. By the end of my shoe-making endeavor, my thumbs were a patchwork of tiny puncture wounds. But the pride I felt in wearing my own handmade sandals far outweighed the discomfort. Even the blisters that formed on my toes from the rough material felt like badges of honor – proof of our ability to adapt and survive.

Our resourcefulness extended to the very tools we used. When needles became scarce, we scavenged old umbrellas, repurposing their metal ribs into makeshift sewing implements. Nothing went to waste. The ropes from the parachutes found new life in the hands of the men, who used them for everything from hauling wood to constructing makeshift barracks.

We children, with our small hands and sharp eyes, became invaluable in this new economy of scarcity. I spent hours combing through piles of discarded items, my heart leaping with joy each time I discovered a usable shoe sole or a piece of material that could be repurposed.

"Look what I found!" I would shout, holding up my prizes for my mother to inspect.

She would smile, a mix of pride and sadness in her eyes. "Well done, Adis. You have a good eye."

These memories, vivid and visceral, are etched deep into my being. The feel of the rough parachute material under my fingers, the ache in my hands after a day of sewing, the triumph of creating something useful out of discarded scraps – these experiences shaped me in ways I'm still discovering.

Years later, when I share these stories, my mother and sister often marvel at the details I recall. "How do you remember all this?" they ask, their own memories softened by time.

But for me, these aren't just memories – they're a part of who I am. They represent not just the hardships we faced, but the incredible resilience and creativity we found within ourselves. In those dark days, we learned that survival wasn't just about enduring – it was about adapting, creating, and finding hope in the smallest victories.

Looking back, I realize that those parachutes brought us more than just supplies. They delivered a powerful lesson: that even in the direst circumstances, human ingenuity can find a way to not just survive but to create and grow. It's a lesson that has stayed with me, a testament to the unbreakable spirit of my people, and a reminder of the strength we all possess when pushed to our limits.

The Scavenger Hunt

In the early morning light, we children would scour the forests, searching for the brown packages that had fallen during the night. It became a game of sorts, a desperate treasure hunt where the prize was survival.

"I found one!" I shouted triumphantly one morning, holding up a small, rectangular package.

Emir rushed over, his eyes wide with excitement. "Is it number six or twelve?" he asked breathlessly.

We both knew that packages six and twelve contained the ultimate prize: M&M candies. As I tore open the wrapper, the smell of chocolate wafted out, and suddenly, I was transported back to my earliest memory - the empty chocolate wrapper I had cherished as a toddler.

"It's just like my wrapper," I whispered, more to myself than to Emir.

"What wrapper?" he asked, confused.

I shook my head, coming back to the present. "Never mind. Let's share these."

As we savored the rare treat, I couldn't help but marvel at how something so simple could bring such joy in these dark times.

A Glimmer of Hope: Mubera's Wedding

In the midst of our struggles, life found a way to remind us of its beauty and resilience. In mid-1994, my second sister Mubera, at the age of 17, got married. Despite the ongoing war, this event brought a rare moment of joy to our family and community.

"It's not much," my mother said, her eyes glistening with a mixture of happiness and sorrow, "but it's a piece of normalcy in these abnormal times."

Unlike Zilka's wedding before the war, Mubera's was a subdued affair, stripped of the traditional fanfare. There were no decorated cars, no fireworks, and no elaborate feast. Instead, a small group of people gathered at our house, bringing what little they could to celebrate. One similarity between the two sisters' marriage was that both had husbands with the same name, Sead.

My cousin, Mesud, a skilled hunter, brought a shoulder of deer he had managed to kill in the forest. This small offering of meat was treated like a precious gift, a reminder of the generosity that still existed even in our dire circumstances.

As I watched Mubera leave with her new husband, I felt a complex mix of emotions. I was happy for her, yet sad to see another sister leave our home. The house felt emptier, but there was comfort in knowing she was marrying into a stable family with more resources than most.

"She'll be okay," my mother assured me, sensing my unease. "And you still have me."

This wedding, humble as it was, gave us all a moment to hope, to believe that life could go on even in the shadow of war. It was a defiant act of normalcy in a world that had become anything but normal.

The Fall of Srebrenica

Our brief moments of happiness were soon overshadowed by grim news from Srebrenica. Refugees began trickling into Žepa, bringing tales of horror and despair that would soon be etched into the annals of history as one of the darkest chapters of the Bosnian War.

One afternoon, a haggard man stumbled into our village. My father approached him, offering water.

"What news from Srebrenica?" he asked gently.

The man's eyes were hollow with fear. "It's fallen," he croaked. "The Serbs... they're killing everyone. The men, the boys... they're all gone."

A chill ran through me as I overheard these words. Žepa and Srebrenica had been twin sanctuaries, both declared 'safe areas' under UN protection. If Srebrenica could fall, what hope did we have?

As July 1995 approached, the horrors we had feared became reality. What would later become known as the Srebrenica massacre or the Srebrenica genocide unfolded with terrifying swiftness. Over 8,000 Bosniak Muslim men and boys were systematically executed in and around the town of Srebrenica. This wasn't just a tragedy; it was the first legally recognized genocide in Europe since the end of World War II.

The betrayal cut deep. The UN Protection Force, a contingent of 370 lightly armed Dutch soldiers, had been overwhelmed and unable to prevent the atrocity. This failure shook our faith in the international community and filled us with dread about our own fate in Žepa. The promise of protection had proven hollow, leaving us to wonder who, if anyone, would stand between us and a similar fate.

The full extent of the massacre was staggering. A list of people missing or killed during the massacre contained 8,372 names. During this siege within Žepa , 457 individuals lost their lives. In the years that followed, painstaking efforts to identify the victims through DNA analysis of body parts recovered from mass graves would reveal the true scale of the atrocity. By 2021, 6,671 bodies had been buried at the Memorial Centre of Potočari, with another 236 buried elsewhere.

The Bosnian Serb Army of Republika Srpska, under the command of Ratko Mladić, bore the primary responsibility for this heinous act. The

Serb paramilitary unit known as the Scorpions also participated in the killings. Some Serbs attempted to justify the massacre as retaliation for earlier casualties inflicted on Serbs by Bosniak soldiers from Srebrenica. However, these claims were unequivocally rejected and condemned by the International Criminal Tribunal for the former Yugoslavia (ICTY) and the UN as bad faith attempts to justify genocide.

The impact of Srebrenica reverberated far beyond our region. In 2004, the Appeals Chamber of the ICTY ruled unanimously that the massacre constituted genocide, a ruling later upheld by the International Court of Justice in 2007. The forcible transfer and abuse of between 25,000 and 30,000 Bosniak Muslim women, children, and elderly, which accompanied the massacre, was also found to constitute genocide when combined with the killings and separation of the men.

The fall of Srebrenica had far-reaching consequences. In 2002, the Dutch government resigned, citing its inability to prevent the massacre. Years later, in 2013, 2014, and 2019, the Dutch state was found liable by its supreme court and the Hague district court for failing to prevent more than 300 deaths.

As we huddled in Žepa, processing the horrifying news from Srebrenica, we couldn't have known that these events would be described by UN Secretary-General Kofi Annan as "a terrible crime – the worst on European soil since the Second World War." We couldn't have imagined that decades later, in 2024, the UN would designate July 11 as the annual International Day of Reflection and Commemoration of the 1995 Genocide in Srebrenica.

For us, in that moment, all we knew was fear. The fall of Srebrenica wasn't just news – it was a dire warning. As we looked at the shell-shocked refugees stumbling into our village, we saw our potential future. The question that hung in the air, unspoken but omnipresent, was chilling: Would Žepa be next?

Losing Mesud

As the war tightened its grip on Žepa, it seemed determined to take not just our freedom, but also those we held dear. In the spring of 1995, just months before the fall of Srebrenica, we lost someone who was more than family to me - my cousin Mesud Ziga.

Mesud and I were bound by blood from both sides of our family. His last name, like mine, was Ziga. On my mother's side, his mom and my grandmother were sisters, while on my father's side, his father and mine shared the same last name—my great-grandfather was his grandfather. This double connection made our bond especially strong, a familial closeness that went beyond mere relation.

I remember the day I heard the news as if it were yesterday. It was a crisp morning, and I was leaving school after a shift change, one of those ordinary moments that would soon be colored by extraordinary grief. The air felt heavy, pregnant with an impending storm that mirrored the turmoil about to unfold in our lives.

"Adis," my father called as I approached our house. His face was ashen, his eyes red-rimmed. "It's Mesud. He's been killed."

The words hit me like a physical blow. Mesud, had been patrolling the outskirts of Žepa. With our forces spread thin, we had to cover vast areas, constantly moving to create the illusion of a larger army and mislead the Serbian forces. It was during one of these patrols that Mesud fell victim to an ambush.

Days passed before they could retrieve his body, the area too dangerous to search immediately. When they finally brought him down from the mountains, the sight seared itself into my memory. They used an old Yugo, one of those iconic Yugoslavian cars, to carry him back to town. I can still see him in the back of that car, the finality of death etched into his still features.

Later, I went to the mosque where they were preparing Mesud for burial. I stood in the corner of the room where they performed the ritual washing of his body, the cold, somber atmosphere a stark contrast to the warmth and life Mesud had always exuded. It wasn't the first time I had confronted death in this war, but seeing someone so close to me, someone who shared my blood and my name, lying there motionless - it affected me in a way I hadn't experienced before.

As I watched the solemn preparations, I thought about all the times Mesud and I had spent together. He had been more than a cousin; he was a friend, a confidant, a link to both sides of my family. His loss left a void that seemed impossible to fill.

In the days that followed, as we mourned Mesud, the atmosphere in Žepa grew even more tense. Rumors swirled about increased Serbian activity, and the fall of Srebrenica loomed on the horizon. Mesud's death became a painful precursor to the larger tragedy that was about to unfold, a personal loss that foreshadowed the communal devastation to come.

As I helped dig Mesud's grave, each shovelful of earth felt like a goodbye not just to my cousin, but to the life we had known. With every passing day, with every life lost, our world was shrinking, our future becoming more uncertain. Mesud's death was a stark reminder of the price we were paying simply for existing, for daring to defend our homes and our right to live.

In the quiet moments after his burial, as the community dispersed and night fell over Žepa, I found myself standing alone by Mesud's fresh grave. The weight of our loss, both personal and collective, pressed down on me. Yet, in that moment of grief, I also felt a renewed determination. Mesud had given his life protecting our home, our people. The least I could do was honor his sacrifice by carrying on, by finding the strength to face whatever challenges lay ahead.

Little did I know then how soon those challenges would come, or how severe they would be. As I walked home that night, the stars hidden behind a veil of smoke from distant shelling, I carried with me not just the memory of Mesud, but the growing realization that our fight for survival was far from over.

The Betrayal

As the days wore on, we watched with growing unease as our Ukrainian peacekeepers began negotiating with the Serbian army. The echoes of Srebrenica's betrayal haunted us all.

"Why are they talking to them?" I asked my father one evening, watching the UN vehicles leave for another round of talks.

He sighed heavily, the weight of the world on his shoulders. "They're trying to find a way out, Adis. For them, and hopefully for us."

But as the negotiations dragged on, it became clear that the Serbs had no intention of allowing a peaceful resolution. The only option they offered was complete surrender.

The Fall of Žepa

As July 1995 progressed, the noose around Žepa tightened inexorably. The distant sounds of shelling grew closer each day, and columns of smoke rose from surrounding villages, grim harbingers of our fate. Only the center of Žepa, my village Štetkov Do, and a couple of others remained untouched, but we knew it was only a matter of time.

Our Ukrainian peacekeepers, who were supposed to protect us, began negotiating with the Serbian army. We watched with growing unease as UN vehicles left for rounds of talks, returning with grim faces and no solutions. The fear that had been simmering for months now reached a boiling point.

The order came suddenly - we were to gather in the center of Žepa to be 'evacuated.' The word hung in the air like a death sentence. As we prepared to leave our homes, possibly for the last time, the reality of our situation hit hard. The life we had known, the community we had built, was coming to an end.

These pictures show Ukrainian UN soldiers posing for a photo, with the burning ruins of Zepa in the background. The structure is specifically Redzep Pasina Kula, built by the Ottomans in 1485.

From the hills surrounding Žepa, we could see Serbian soldiers entering the outlying villages. The sound of gunfire grew closer each day. Families rushed to gather what few possessions they could carry. I watched my mother move through our house with quiet determination, her face a mask of stoic resolve as she decided what to take and what to leave behind.

In those final days, a surreal atmosphere settled over Žepa. Children played in the streets, their laughter a jarring counterpoint to the fear etched on every adult face. Neighbors gathered to share what little food remained, a last communion of a community about to be scattered to the winds.

The smoke from burning houses formed a dark canopy over our once-peaceful valley. It was clear that Žepa's fall was imminent, and with it, the last vestiges of our normal lives would be consumed by the insatiable appetite of war. As night fell on what would be our last evening in Žepa, I looked out over the town, trying to burn every detail into my memory, knowing that the Žepa I knew would soon exist only in our memories and hearts.

The Chaos of Escape

The news came suddenly, spreading through our village like wildfire. Our leaders, who had been negotiating with the Serbian Army, relayed urgent orders: we were to make our way to the mountain immediately. Helicopters, we were told, would be waiting there to transport us to safety in Sarajevo. The message ignited a spark of hope in our weary hearts but also set off a frantic scramble as families hurried to gather what little they could carry.

In a desperate bid for survival, we fled to the mountains. It was a grueling journey, a steep three-kilometer hike that tested our already depleted strength. The path was treacherous, made worse by the panic and confusion that surrounded us. My sister Zilka struggled up the path, carrying her infant daughter. In her exhaustion and the chaos of our flight, she unknowingly held the child upside down for much of the climb. When we finally reached the top, we were horrified to find the baby blue-faced and barely breathing. It was a terrifying reminder of how easily tragedy could strike in our chaotic escape.

Our relief at reaching the supposed safety of the mountain was short-lived. As we arrived, gasping for breath and searching the skies, the cruel truth became apparent - there were no helicopters waiting for us. The promise of evacuation to Sarajevo had been a false hope, perhaps a miscommunication or a plan that had fallen through in the unpredictable chaos of war.

Instead of salvation, we found only crushing disappointment and new orders that sent waves of fear through the crowd. We were told we had to go back. But this return wasn't a simple retracing of our steps. A new, heartbreaking decision had to be made.

The message from our leaders, still negotiating with the Serbian Army, was clear but devastating: women and children were to make their way to Žepa, while the men were to stay behind. This order came in the wake of the horrors we had heard about in Srebrenica. The Serbs wanted everyone, including the men, to surrender. But we knew all too well what that could mean.

It was in this moment of crushing disappointment and terrible clarity that we said goodbye to my father. The decision was agonizing but necessary. He, like many other men, knew that returning to the village meant certain capture or death. The fate of the men of Srebrenica hung heavily over this choice. My father, along with countless others, chose to stay behind on the mountain rather than face what seemed like certain doom below.

As we prepared to separate, the gravity of our situation bore down upon us. Families were being torn apart, with no certainty of reunion. The mountain, which had briefly represented hope, now became a symbol of our desperate last stand. For the women and children, the journey ahead to Žepa promised its own perils. For the men staying behind, an uncertain fate awaited.

This moment of parting, fraught with fear, love, and desperate hope, would be etched into our memories forever. It was more than just a physical journey down the mountain; it was a descent into an unknown future, carrying the weight of our loved ones' fates on our shoulders.

The Parting

I'll never forget that moment on the mountain, a scene that would haunt my dreams for years to come. My father, still in civilian clothes, stood apart from the group of men who had decided to stay behind. His face was etched with a mixture of determination and sorrow as he hugged us all goodbye.

"Be strong, my son," he said, embracing me fiercely. "Take care of your mother and sisters." His voice cracked slightly, betraying the emotion he was trying to hide.

My mother cried silently, but no tears came – perhaps she had none left to shed after years of hardship. Her eyes, usually so full of warmth, now held a distant, haunted look. She clutched my hand tightly, as if afraid I too might disappear if she let go.

As we began our descent, I kept looking back, watching my father's figure grow smaller until he disappeared from view. The mist swirling around the mountaintop seemed to swallow him whole, along with the other men who stayed behind. I didn't know then that the next time I would see him, he would be in full military attire, a transformation symbolic of how the war had changed us all.

My brother-in-law, Sead, initially came down the mountain with us. He walked beside my sister Zilka, who was still shaken from the incident with her baby on the climb up. His arm was around her, supporting her both physically and emotionally. I could see the conflict in his eyes – the desire to protect his family warring with the knowledge of what awaited men who returned to the village.

As we approached Žepa, the distant sound of engines grew louder. Through the trees, we could see Serbian soldiers loading people onto buses. The sight sent a chill through our group. Sead stopped walking, his face a mask of anguish.

"I can't go any further," he said, his voice barely above a whisper. "If I do, I might never see you again."

With a heart-wrenching goodbye, he hugged Zilka and kissed his child. Then, casting one last longing look at his family, he turned and ventured back into the forest, towards the uncertain safety of the mountains.

We stood there for a moment, watching him disappear into the trees, just as we had watched my father vanish into the mist. In the span of a few hours, we had been torn apart, our family scattered by the cruel winds of war. As we continued our descent towards an uncertain fate, I felt the weight of my father's words pressing down on me. I was just a boy, but in that moment, I knew I had to find the strength of a man.

After the war, more tragedy awaited. My brother-in-law, along with my uncles, were captured and held in a concentration camp for about 10 months, from the summer of 1995 to late spring of '96. During this time, my father was struggling to reach free territory through the forests, developing PTSD that would haunt him for years to come.

The Final Journey

"What will happen to Babo?" I asked my mother, voicing the fear that had been gnawing at me since we left the mountain.

She pulled me close, her voice low but firm. "Your father is strong and clever, Adis. He will find a way to survive, and we will be reunited. We must have faith."

I nodded, trying to draw strength from her words, even as I saw the worry etched in the lines of her face.

We returned to find our family home overflowing with people. My mother, ever compassionate, broke into bedrooms to gather blankets and pillows for those forced to sleep on the ground. As she rummaged through Zilka's room, I noticed a pile of school books and notebooks on the floor.

One book caught my eye – a familiar chocolate wrapper peeking out from between its pages. I carefully extracted the makeshift bookmark, bringing it to my nose. The faint cocoa scent transported me back to a sweeter time when Zilka and I had shared that very chocolate bar, giggling over a silly, childish joke we had shared. I crinkled the wrapper between my fingers, savoring the memory. The sound seemed to echo in the crowded room, a stark reminder of how our once-peaceful home had become a refuge for strangers fleeing the war. That night, we watched helplessly as more villages burned. My sister wept as she saw the cabin she and her husband had built during the war go up in flames – another dream consumed by the insatiable appetite of conflict.

The next morning, we were ordered to the center of Žepa for evacuation. It was chaos. Women cried, clinging to UN vehicles, begging the peacekeepers not to leave. We knew that once they were gone, our last shield against the Serbian forces would be gone.

Amidst the confusion, a Serbian soldier grabbed me. He positioned me on a small brick wall near the town's fountain – a place once a symbol of community gatherings, now a stage for propaganda. He instructed me to smile and look towards the mountains while he took photos. I later learned these images were used to portray a false narrative of happy, willing evacuees.

As buses filled and departed, our numbers dwindled. We watched them wind up the mountain road – the same road that once brought us hope in the form of aid convoys, now carrying our people away to an uncertain fate. We didn't know then that for many, especially in Srebrenica, these buses were heading to slaughter.

As we were loaded onto an 18-wheeler truck, I clung to a small jar of honey my mother had found near our neighborhood, my last connection to home. The journey that followed was a nightmare of heat, thirst, and fear. Serbian soldiers would stop the trucks periodically, climbing on top to terrorize us. They would disrespect women by pulling down their scarves, slapping crying babies, and subjecting us to other harsh treatments. Their cruelty seemed to know no bounds as they sought to humiliate and terrorize us at every opportunity.

"Turk bastards!" they would shout, striking out at random with their rifle butts.

I huddled closer to my mother, trying to make myself invisible. The honey jar was warm in my hands, a reminder of sweeter times.

Reflecting Back

As I write these words now, decades removed from those harrowing days, the memories still have the power to overwhelm me. The fall of Žepa marked the end of my childhood in many ways. In the span of a few days, I had said goodbye to my father, left behind the only home I had ever known, and faced terrors no child should ever have to endure.

Yet amid the darkness, there were moments of light - the solidarity of our community, the unwavering love and strength of my mother, and the small acts of kindness that reminded us of our humanity. The jar of honey I carried throughout that journey became a symbol of resilience, a taste of home that sustained us through the bitterest times.

Today, as I watch my nieces and nephews grow up in peace and plenty, universally speaking, I am acutely aware of how fragile that peace can be. The lessons of Žepa - of courage, of perseverance, of the strength found in unity - are ones I strive to pass on to them. For in the end, it is not the horrors we faced that define us, but how we faced them, and how we rebuilt our lives in the aftermath.

The empty chocolate wrapper of my childhood, once a symbol of deprivation, now represents something different to me. It reminds me of the power of hope, of finding joy in the smallest things, and of the unbreakable spirit of a people determined to survive. I dedicate my shared story to those who did not survive, in hope that the world does not need reminders on the human cost of hatred and division.

Writing and rewriting these stories have reminded me of what and who I should be thankful - for the sacrifices of my parents, for the strength of my community, and for the chance to build a new life. As I am thankful, I also feel a weight of responsibility - to remember, bear witness, and keep working towards a world where no child has to experience what we all did in Žepa.

CHAPTER 5

Post Exodus: The Long Walk to Freedom

Dumped into Dawn

As the trucks ground to a halt, the sudden silence was deafening. The back doors swung open, flooding the cramped space with the pale light of dawn. A harsh voice barked out orders in Serbian.

"Out! Everyone out! Move!"

We stumbled from the truck, our legs weak from the long, cramped journey. The cool morning air hit my face, a stark contrast to the stifling heat we'd endured for hours. As my eyes adjusted to the light, I took in our surroundings. We were on a road, but nature had begun to reclaim it. Trees encroached from both sides, their branches forming a canopy overhead.

My mother's hand found mine, gripping it tightly. "Stay close, Adis," she whispered, her voice trembling slightly.

I nodded, clutching the jar of honey I'd managed to keep throughout our journey. It felt like the last tangible connection to our home in Žepa.

The Misty Path

We were herded forward by the Serbian soldiers, their rifles pointed at our backs. The morning mist clung to everything, giving the scene an eerie, dreamlike quality. Under different circumstances, it might have been beautiful – the kind of morning you'd wake up early to enjoy in peace. But there was no peace here, only the shuffling of hundreds of feet and the occasional cry of a child.

As we walked, I couldn't help but notice how the road had changed. Once a main thoroughfare, it was now overgrown, nature slowly erasing the signs of human presence. It felt like we were walking through a forgotten world.

"Keep moving!" a soldier shouted, his voice cutting through the fog.

I glanced at my sister Zilka, walking a few paces ahead with her baby. The child had been mercifully quiet since we left the truck, perhaps sensing the tension in the air.

Ambush in the Woods

We had been walking for what felt like hours when suddenly, the quiet was shattered. Three Serbian soldiers burst from the woods, their sudden appearance sending a ripple of fear through the column of refugees.

One soldier, a red bandana tied around his head and a long knife hanging from his belt, began grabbing people at random. "Watches! Jewelry! Hand it over!" he snarled.

Another soldier held a basket, which was quickly filling with the meager valuables of the refugees. The third stood watch, his rifle ready.

I watched in horror as they made their way through the crowd, snatching earrings from women's ears, and pulling rings from trembling fingers. Those who had nothing visible to give were roughly searched, the soldiers' hands probing for hidden treasures.

As they approached us, I saw my sister Zilka tighten her grip on her baby. The child, perhaps sensing her mother's fear, began to cry.

One of the soldiers, his face twisted with anger, strode towards Zilka. "Shut that brat up," he growled, "or I'll throw it down the canyon myself!"

I followed his gaze to the steep drop-off beside the road, my heart pounding. Surely he wouldn't...

Zilka clutched baby Selma tighter, nearly smothering the child in her desperation to quiet her. Miraculously, the baby's cries subsided to whimpers.

The soldier turned his attention to my mother and me. "Money," he demanded, his eyes cold. "Jewelry. Now."

My mother shook her head. "We have nothing," she said, her voice barely above a whisper.

Salvation in a Moment of Terror

The soldier's eyes narrowed as he looked at my mother, then at me. "Well," he sneered, "you may not have anything, but you have this boy. He'll grow up to be a strong soldier someday."

Without warning, he grabbed me, pulling me away from my mother. I felt the cold steel of his knife press against my throat, and terror gripped me.

"You have him," the soldier growled again, his voice filled with hate. He turned to my mother, spewing derogatory names at her, calling her a "Turkish whore" and other vulgar terms I had never heard before.

The word 'Turkish' stung in a way I couldn't fully comprehend at the time. Later, I would come to understand the weight and history behind this slur. The Serb soldiers, as part of their campaign of ethnic cleansing, referred to us Bosniaks (Bosnian Muslims) as 'Turks'. This wasn't merely an insult; it was a calculated attempt to delegitimize our presence in Bosnia.

By calling us 'Turks', they were pushing a narrative that we didn't belong in Bosnia, that we were somehow foreign invaders rather than native inhabitants. This rhetoric ignored centuries of history, disregarding the fact that our ancestors had lived on this land long before they embraced Islam. It was a cruel irony - the very people threatening to expel us from our homes were claiming we were the outsiders.

This language was part of a broader strategy of dehumanization. By painting us as 'Turks', they attempted to separate us from our Bosnian identity, to make it easier for their soldiers to commit atrocities against us. It was a form of psychological warfare, aimed at both breaking our spirits and justifying their actions to themselves and the world.

As I stood there, a child with a knife at my throat, I couldn't grasp the complex history behind the soldier's words. All I knew was the fear, the confusion, and the desperate look in my mother's eyes. In that moment, the weight of centuries of conflict, of identities imposed and denied, bore down on us with the cold press of a blade.

I felt the knife press harder, and a whimper escaped my lips. My mother's face went pale, her eyes wide with terror.

"Please," she begged, "I swear, we have nothing. Please, don't hurt my son!"

My mother's face paled, her composure cracking for a moment. "Please," she begged, her voice trembling. "I'm telling you, I don't have anything. Please don't hurt my son."

The soldier, still holding me with the knife at my throat, began roughly searching my mother. His free hand snatched at her clothes, feeling for hidden pockets. I remembered how my mother sometimes hid things in the bottom of her hand-knitted vests, a traditional Bosnian trick for keeping valuables safe. But this time, there was nothing to find.

Desperate, my mother reached into her bag. "This is all I have," she said, her voice barely above a whisper. "I really don't have anything else. Please, don't do anything to my son."

She opened her hand, revealing a small golden trinket. The soldier didn't even touch it, just gestured to the basket. "Put it in there," he ordered gruffly.

As my mother complied, the soldier maintained his grip on me. Then, suddenly, he shoved my mother roughly. She stumbled but kept her eyes on me, pleading, "Please let him go. Please let him go."

The crowd of refugees continued to move around us, creating a pressure that seemed to frustrate the soldier. In a sudden motion, he snatched me away from himself and shoved me towards my mother.

I stumbled into her arms, still clutching the jar of honey I had somehow managed to hold onto throughout this ordeal. As my mother pulled me close, I looked back to see the soldier already grabbing another person, continuing his cruel search for valuables.

"Keep going, keep going," my mother urged, her hand on the back of my head, forcing me to look forward. "Don't look back, Adis. Just keep walking."

We moved forward with the crowd, my mother's arm protectively around me, the jar of honey still clutched in my hands - a small, sweet reminder of home amidst the bitterness of our exodus.

The Long Walk Continues

We continued our journey, the forest gradually thinning out. In the distance, I could make out the shape of a building – a hotel, I realized, remembering stories I'd heard of the area.

As we passed, I saw more soldiers milling about. Some were pulling people aside, for what purpose I didn't know and didn't want to imagine. My mother kept her eyes forward, her grip on my hand never loosening.

The Tunnel of Hope

After what seemed like an eternity of walking, we saw it – the mouth of a tunnel stretching before us. On the other side, barely visible in the distance, were figures in different uniforms. Bosnian soldiers.

A murmur of relief passed through the crowd. We were almost there. Almost safe.

As we entered the tunnel, the darkness enveloped us. The sound of our footsteps echoed off the walls, creating a cacophony of shuffling and whispers. I clung to my mother, fear and hope warring within me.

"We're almost there, Adis," my mother whispered. "Just a little further."

Emerging into Light

When we finally emerged from the other side of the tunnel, the sunlight was blinding. As my eyes adjusted, I saw them – Bosnian soldiers, their familiar uniforms a welcome sight after days of fear.

One soldier approached us, his face etched with concern. "Welcome," he said, his voice gentle. "You're safe now."

The tension that had held us rigid for so long began to dissipate. Around me, I could hear sobs of relief, and cries of joy as families realized they had made it through together.

The Refugee Camp

We were directed to a large open area where tents had been set up. It was chaotic, with people rushing about, calling out names, searching for loved ones. The sheer number of strangers around us was overwhelming, a sea of unfamiliar faces all sharing the same look of confusion and fear.

My mother turned to me, her eyes filled with determination. "Adis, I need you to watch Selma for a while. Can you do that for me?"

I nodded, taking my young niece from Zilka's arms. "Where are you going?" I asked, trying to keep the worry from my voice.

"We're going to look for the rest of our family," my mother explained. "Stay here. We'll be back soon."

As they disappeared into the crowd, I held Selma close, feeling suddenly very small and alone in the vast, chaotic camp. The baby whimpered softly, perhaps sensing my unease.

"It's okay," I whispered, as much to myself as to her. "They'll be back soon."

Time seemed to stretch endlessly as I waited, watching the constant movement of people around us. I tried to distract Selma by making funny faces, grateful for the momentary escape from our grim reality.

Finally, after what felt like hours, I spotted my mother and Zilka making their way back to us. Their faces wore expressions of relief that I hadn't seen in a long time.

"Adis," my mother called as they approached. "We found them!"

"Who?" I asked, hope rising in my chest.

"Your Nana Bahija," she said, smiling. "And Aunt Raza with your cousins. We even found Uncle Emin's wife and their three children."

The news washed over me like a warm wave. We weren't alone. Our family, or at least part of it, was here and safe.

As if summoned by our conversation, familiar faces began to appear. My grandmother Bahija arrived first, her eyes filling with tears as she saw us.

"Adis! Ramiza!" she cried, rushing forward to embrace us.

As she held me tight, I could feel her body shaking with sobs. "Thank Allah you're safe," she murmured, her voice thick with emotion.

More reunions followed - tearful, joyful encounters that seemed miraculous given what we had all been through. As the initial shock of seeing each other wore off, we gathered in and around our assigned tent, creating a small island of familiarity in the sea of strangers.

To my surprise, I found myself relaxing a bit. The presence of family, and the sound of familiar voices, eased some of the tension that had been my constant companion for so long.

My cousins and I, drawn together by a shared experience we were too young to fully comprehend, began to play. We explored our new surroundings, examined the food rations we'd been given - so similar to the aid packages we'd received in Žepa - and for brief moments, we managed to forget where we were and why.

As I chased my younger cousin around the tent, laughing for what felt like the first time in ages, I caught my mother watching us, a bittersweet smile on her face. Perhaps she, like me, was grateful for this small moment of normalcy amidst the chaos.

We were still refugees, still displaced, and facing an uncertain future. But in that moment, playing with my cousins under the watchful eyes of our family, I felt a flicker of hope. We had survived. We were together. And somehow, we would find a way forward.

Reunions and Revelations

Over the next few hours, more family members found their way to us. Cousins, aunts, uncles – each reunion was a mixture of joy and sorrow as we shared our experiences and counted those still missing.

My mother, finally allowing herself to relax slightly, reached into her coat. To my surprise, she pulled out a small wad of German marks.

"I forgot I had these," she said, her voice filled with wonder and guilt. "Your father gave them to me before... before we left."

I remembered the soldier with the knife, and how close we had come to disaster. But I couldn't blame my mother. The fear and confusion of our flight had muddled all our minds.

"It doesn't matter now, Majka," I said, hugging her tightly. "We're here. We're safe."

The New Reality

As night fell on the refugee camp, the initial relief of our arrival gave way to a new set of worries. Where would we go from here? What had happened to those left behind – my father, my brother-in-law, and so many others?

I lay on a thin blanket, staring up at the tent ceiling. The sounds of the camp – muffled conversations, occasional cries, the rustle of movement – created a strange lullaby.

Next to me, my mother slept fitfully, her face etched with lines of worry even in sleep. My sister Zilka cradled baby Selma, humming softly to soothe the child – or perhaps herself.

As I drifted off to sleep, my last thoughts were of Žepa, of our home, of my father. In the morning, I knew we would face a new chapter in our lives as refugees. But for now, in this moment, we were alive. We were together. And somehow, against all odds, we had hope.

Reflections on Freedom

In the days that followed, the refugee camp became our new, temporary home. It was a place of contradictions – relief mixed with anxiety, joy at reunions tempered by grief for those lost or left behind.

I remember watching my mother in those early days, marveling at her strength. Despite everything we had been through, she worked tirelessly to create a sense of normalcy for us. She would rise early, queuing for our daily rations, then return to our tent to prepare what meager meal she could.

"Eat, Adis," she would say, pushing the best portions towards me. "You need to keep up your strength."

I would protest, trying to give it back, but she would insist. It was in these small acts of sacrifice that I truly began to understand the depth of a parent's love.

The camp was a melting pot of stories. In the evenings, people would gather, sharing their experiences of the exodus. Some tales were heartbreaking – families separated, loved ones lost. Others were inspiring – acts of bravery, moments of unexpected kindness from strangers.

One evening, an old man from a village near Žepa told us how a Serbian family had hidden him in their cellar for days, risking their own lives to save his. "Even in the darkest times," he said, his eyes glistening with tears, "humanity can shine through."

These stories became our sustenance, reminding us of the resilience of the human spirit. They gave us hope that even after all we had endured, there was still good in the world.

Uncertain Futures

As days turned into weeks, the initial shock of our displacement began to wear off, replaced by a gnawing uncertainty about our future. Rumors swirled through the camp – of cities willing to take refugees, of countries offering asylum, of the ongoing war and the fates of those left behind.

One afternoon, I overheard my mother talking with my aunt in hushed tones.

"What will we do, Ramiza?" my aunt asked, her voice trembling. "Where will we go?"

My mother was silent for a moment before responding. "We go where we must," she said firmly. "We do what we need to survive. For our children."

I pretended to be asleep, but her words echoed in my mind. Once again, we would have to leave everything behind, to start anew in a place we didn't know.

That night, as I lay awake listening to the sounds of the camp, I thought about all we had lost – our home, our community, the life we had known. But we had gained something too – a fierce determination to survive, to honor those we had lost by living, by remembering.

As sleep finally claimed me, I held onto that thought. Whatever came next, whatever challenges we faced, we would face them together. We had survived the fall of Žepa, the terror of exodus. We were stronger than we knew.

In the darkness of the refugee tent, on the cusp of an uncertain future, I found myself whispering the words my father had said to me what felt like a lifetime ago: "We are Bosnians. We are strong. And we will never give up.

CHAPTER 6

The Long Road to Reunion

The Hero of Žepa

As we prepared to leave Žepa, my young mind struggled to comprehend the enormity of what was happening. Amidst the chaos and fear, one name stood out - Avdo Palić. He was a man I had seen around town, always with a kind word or reassuring smile for everyone, even in the darkest times.

Avdo Palić was more than just a military officer; he was the heart and soul of our resistance in Žepa. At 37 years old, he had already lived a lifetime of experiences. Once a respected officer in the Yugoslav People's Army, he had made the difficult decision to desert when the war broke out, choosing to stand with his people rather than against them.

I remember overhearing my father and other men talking about him in hushed, reverent tones. "Palić is negotiating with the Serbs," they'd say. "If anyone can get us out of this, it's him."

As we gathered on the mountain, waiting for the helicopters that would never come, word spread that Avdo Palić had made a deal. He would ensure the safe evacuation of all civilians, but at a terrible cost - he would be the last to leave Žepa.

"He's sacrificing himself for us." my mother whispered, her voice thick with emotion.

I didn't fully understand then what that meant, but I could feel the weight of his decision in the air around us. As we began our descent back to the town, I caught a glimpse of Avdo Palić. He stood tall, his face a mask of determination, as he shook hands with the Serbian commanders.

Little did we know that this would be the last time many of us would see him alive.

The Search for Answers

Despite the joy of our reunions, a cloud of uncertainty hung over us. We had no news of my father, my brother-in-law, or many other men from Žepa. Each day, my sister Zilka would make the trek to the camp's information center, hoping for any word of their fate.

"Anything?" I would ask eagerly each time she returned.

For days, the answer was always the same - a sad shake of the head, a quiet "Not yet." But Zilka never gave up. Every morning, she would set out again, determined to find some news.

One evening, as we sat around our small camp stove, I overheard my mother and aunt talking in hushed tones.

"What do you think happened to Avdo Palić?" my aunt asked.

My mother sighed heavily. "I don't know. But he saved us all. Whatever his fate, he's a hero."

I thought back to that last glimpse I'd had of Avdo Palić, standing tall as he shook hands with the Serbian commanders. In that moment, he had seemed invincible. Now, I understood the true cost of his bravery.

Years later, we would learn the tragic truth. Avdo Palić had indeed sacrificed everything for us. He was executed shortly after ensuring our safe passage. His remains wouldn't be found until 2001, and it would take until 2009 for his family to finally be able to lay him to rest.

The legacy of Avdo Palić lived on in all of us who escaped Žepa. His courage had bought us a chance at survival, a debt we could never repay but would always remember.

Moving On

After several days in the refugee camp, word came that we were to be moved again. The camp was overcrowded, and authorities were trying to distribute refugees to different parts of Bosnia that could accommodate them.

"We're going to Zenica," my mother told us one evening. "It's a big industrial city. Your sister's father-in-law is there. At least we'll know someone."

The news brought a mix of emotions. On one hand, the prospect of leaving the crowded camp was appealing. On the other, it meant another journey into the unknown.

The next morning, we found ourselves boarding a cargo train. The car was little more than a metal box on wheels, but it was taking us away from the limbo of the refugee camp and towards... what? We didn't know, but we had to believe it would be better.

As the train lurched into motion, I pressed my face against a small gap in the wall, watching the landscape roll by. The countryside was beautiful, untouched by the ravages of war that had scarred so much of our homeland. For a moment, I could almost pretend we were on a normal journey, not fleeing for our lives.

"What do you think Zenica will be like?" I asked my mother.

She smiled, running her hand through my hair. "I don't know, Adis. But we'll face it together, as we always have."

Arrival in Zenica

The train journey seemed endless, but finally, we arrived in Zenica. As we disembarked, I was struck by the bustle of the city. After so long in Žepa and then the refugee camp, the sight of a functioning urban center was almost overwhelming.

We were met by my sister's father-in-law, hobbling towards us on crutches. His missing leg was a stark reminder of the price so many had paid in this war. He embraced Zilka tightly, tears in his eyes.

"I'm so glad you're safe," he said, his voice choked with emotion. "But I'm afraid I can't take you all in. There's just no room."

My heart sank at his words, but before despair could take hold, he continued.

"But don't worry. They're setting up temporary housing for refugees. It's not much, but it's something."

And so we found ourselves in an old movie theater, the seats removed to make space for rows of foam mattresses. It was far from ideal, but after everything we'd been through, it felt like luxury.

As we settled in, I noticed my mother talking with a group of women. Her face was animated, her hands gesturing as she spoke. When she returned to our little corner, she was smiling.

"What is it, Majka?" I asked.

"Good news, Adis," she replied. "They're offering to help locals renovate unused spaces - attics, basements - if they'll house refugees. We might have a real roof over our heads soon."

Hope, that fragile thing that had sustained us through so much, flared anew. We weren't home, not yet. But we were safe, we were together, and for now, that was enough.

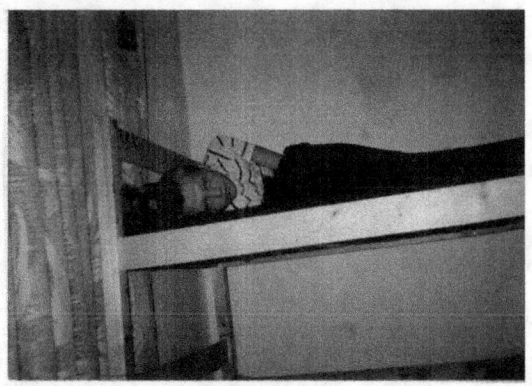

A snapshot of me at the refugee camp in Zenica, 1995.

The Taste of Normalcy

Life in Zenica took on a routine of sorts. Each day brought new challenges, but also small joys that seemed magnified after our ordeal. One of my clearest memories from this time was the discovery of vanilla pudding.

It was part of our rations, a small plastic cup of creamy sweetness that seemed like the height of luxury after months of deprivation. The first time I tasted it, I couldn't believe something so delicious could exist in our new, harsh reality.

"Majka, have you tried this?" I asked, offering her a spoonful.

She smiled, shaking her head. "You enjoy it, Adis. You deserve a treat."

I savored every spoonful and soon found myself trading with other children for their vanilla puddings. It became a bright spot in our days, a small taste of normalcy in a world turned upside down.

Even now, years later, the taste of vanilla pudding takes me back to that movie theater in Zenica, to the mix of hardship and hope that defined those days.

A New Home

After a week in the movie theater, we were moved to the outskirts of Zenica, to an area known as Gornja Zenica. Our new home was an old clay house, built in the traditional cob style with mud bricks reinforced with straw.

The owner, an old communist named Salim, welcomed us warmly. The house was filled with relics of Yugoslavia's past - pictures of Tito, party pins, books extolling the virtues of socialism. To Salim, these weren't just decorations, but treasured symbols of a time he clearly missed.

As we settled into our new quarters, I couldn't help but explore. The house was a treasure trove of history, each room telling a story of a Yugoslavia that no longer existed. It was a stark contrast to the war-torn world outside, a reminder of the peace we had lost and hoped to regain.

The Waiting Game

Life in Gornja Zenica settled into a routine, but always, always, there was the undercurrent of worry about my father. Each day, Zilka would make the long walk into town to check for news at the Red Cross station.

I could see the worry in her eyes, the fear she tried so hard to hide from us. Each night, I would fall asleep to the sound of her quiet prayers, pleading for my father's safe return.

As the days turned to weeks, and the weeks to months, I found myself scanning every face I saw, hoping against hope to see my father. But always, there was disappointment.

Finding Mubera

Amidst the chaos of our arrival and the overwhelming task of rebuilding our lives in Zenica, there was one bright spot that gave us hope - we finally learned the whereabouts of my sister Mubera. For several agonizing months since our separation due to the war, we had no idea where she was or if she was even alive. The uncertainty had been a constant weight on our hearts, especially for my mother. But now, as we waited for my father and brother-in-law to arrive, we received the news we had been desperately praying for.

Mubera was alive and safe in the city of Visoko. She was living with her in-laws in newly built temporary housing. The relief that washed over us was indescribable. It was as if a missing piece of our family puzzle had finally been found. Despite the hardships we still faced, knowing that Mubera was safe gave us renewed strength. It was a reminder that even in the darkest times, there could be moments of joy and reunion. The thought of seeing her again, of our family being whole once more, became a beacon of hope as we navigated our new life in Zenica.

The New Normal

Despite the constant worry, life had to go on. My mother, refusing to be idle, found work in the fields around our new home. She put her green thumb to use, coaxing life from the soil even as winter approached.

I was enrolled in school, put back a grade due to the time I had missed. The other children, with their nice clothes and uninterrupted educations, seemed like creatures from another world. But I was determined to catch up, to make my parents proud.

One morning, as I prepared for school, my mother fussed over my mismatched, donated clothes. She smoothed my hair and straightened my collar, her touch full of love and pride.

"Remember, Adis," she said, her eyes meeting mine, "it's not what you wear that matters, but who you are inside. You are strong, you are smart, and you are loved. Never forget that."

Her words stayed with me as I walked to school, my head held high despite my patched clothes. We had survived so much, my family and I. Whatever challenges lay ahead, I knew we would face them together.

And always, always, we held onto the hope that one day soon, our family would be whole again.

CHAPTER 7

Reunions and New Beginnings

A Dawn of Hope

The early morning mist clung to the flowers lining the pathway as I burst out of our small house in Gornja Zenica. My heart pounded with a mixture of excitement and disbelief. Could it really be true?

My mother's words still echoed in my ears: "Adis, wake up. He's here. Your father is here."

At first, I couldn't comprehend her words, my mind sluggish from sleep. "Who's here, Majka?" I had mumbled.

But as her words sank in, I felt a surge of energy. My father, who we hadn't seen since that terrible day on the mountain in Žepa, was alive and had found us.

The Long-Awaited Reunion

My father after our reunion in Zenica year 1995. This was the first time I saw my father after the fall of Žepa.

I raced down the flower-lined path, my bare feet barely touching the dew-covered grass. As I reached the main street, I saw a group of people gathered near the retirement home where many refugees were staying. Their voices were a distant buzz; I was focused on one thing only - finding my father.

As I rounded the corner, I saw him. Through the morning mist, a figure approached, dressed in full military uniform. For a moment, I hesitated. This man looked so different from the father I remembered - the civilian, the lumberjack. But as he drew closer, I recognized the familiar mustache, the dark curly hair, the warm eyes that had comforted me through so many hardships. I couldn't help admire how handsome he looked.

"Babo!" I cried out, my voice cracking with emotion.

He opened his arms wide, and I ran into them. The familiar scent of him - a mixture of pine and smoke - filled my nostrils, bringing back a flood of memories.

"Adis, sine moj, Adis, my son," he said, his voice thick with emotion. "Look at how you've grown!"

I stepped back, suddenly aware that I was indeed taller. My eyes now reached his shoulders, no longer level with his chest as they had been when we last embraced.

"Are you alright?" he asked, his eyes scanning me for any signs of harm. "Were you hurt? Your mother, your sisters?"

I shook my head, not trusting my voice to speak. There would be time later to share our stories and the hardships we had endured. For now, it was enough to have him here, solid and real before me.

A Family Whole Again

I heard footsteps behind me and turned to see my mother and sister approaching, Zilka carrying Selma. My father's eyes widened as he took in the sight of his family.

"Ahmo," my mother whispered as we all moved closer to each other, with arms stretched out.

"Raha," he breathed, reaching out to my mother. They embraced tightly, years of worry and separation dissolving in that moment.

As they parted, my father turned to Zilka and Selma. "My girl," he said softly, touching Zilka's cheek. Then he looked at Selma, who was regarding him with curious eyes. "And you, little one. You've grown so much."

Our reunion drew attention of the other refugees. Soon, we were surrounded by people, all eager for news. "Have you seen my son?" "Do you know what happened to my husband?" The questions came rapid-fire, each person hoping for news of their loved ones.

My father answered as best he could, offering what information he had about those who had survived the journey through the forests. Some responses brought joy, others tears. It was a stark reminder that while our family was whole again, many others were still fractured by the war.

The Soldier's Tale

As we made our way back to our temporary home, my father began to share bits and pieces of his journey. The full story would come later, but even these fragments painted a picture of hardship and survival that left me in awe.

"We split into two groups," he explained. "Some went towards Serbia, hoping to cross the Drina and reach Goražde. We headed towards Sarajevo, through Han Pijesak, and over Mount Romanija."

I listened, wide-eyed, as he described ambushes, nights spent in freezing forests, and close calls with Serbian patrols. His voice grew quiet as he spoke of lost comrades, men who hadn't survived the journey.

"We made it through because we knew the land," he said, a note of pride in his voice. "Those years working in the lumber company, they saved our lives."

Looking at my father now, it was hard to reconcile the hardships he described with his appearance. He looked healthier than when we'd last seen him, his face fuller, his posture strong. But I could see the toll of his experiences in his eyes - a new wariness, a depth of sadness that hadn't been there before.

Life in Gornja Zenica

Zenica settled into a new rhythm with my father's return. Though the challenges of refugee life persisted—the cramped quarters, the reliance on aid, the looming uncertainty about what the future held—his presence brought a measure of stability that had been sorely missing. His return filled a void, anchoring us in ways that words alone could not.

Each time we visited Žepa , he would show me a little more of the path they had taken—navigating roads and fields under the cover of darkness to reach free territory. These stories, spoken in fragments and gestures, were like pieces of a puzzle that I could never fully assemble but still felt compelled to understand.

As I watched my father attempt to acclimate to civilian life, I noticed how the war lingered in his every movement. There were moments when he seemed lost, his gaze fixed on something distant and unreachable. Sudden noises would startle him, his body instinctively tensing, as if bracing for an unseen threat. Yet no matter how deeply the past tugged at him, he always found a way to shake it off, his face softening into a reassuring smile for those around him. That smile, I realized, was his way of protecting us, a shield between his private battles and the fragile sense of normalcy he worked so hard to rebuild.

One evening, as we sat around our small table, my mother finally shared the full story of our escape from Žepa - including the terrifying encounter with the Serbian soldier who had held a knife to my throat.

I watched my father's face as she spoke, and saw the play of emotions - anger, fear, guilt - before he managed to school his features into a calm mask. When she finished, he reached out and took her hand, then mine.

"I'm so sorry I wasn't there to protect you," he said, his voice rough with emotion. "But I'm so proud of how brave you both were. How brave you all were."

News of the Other Group

While we rejoiced in my father's return, we still worried about those who had taken the other route out of Žepa - including my brother-in-law, Sead, and my uncle Osmo. For weeks, we had no news of their fate.

Then one day, Zilka returned from her daily trip to the Red Cross station with a spark of hope in her eyes. "I found a note from Sead," she announced, her voice trembling with emotion. "He's alive. In a prison camp, but alive."

The news was bittersweet. While we were relieved to know Sead had survived, the thought of him in a prison camp was horrifying. And still, we had no word of my uncle or the others who had gone that way.

As the days passed, more information trickled in. We learned that many of the men who had attempted to cross into Serbia had been captured and sent to concentration camps - Sljivovica and Mitrovo Polje. The stories that reached us of conditions in these camps were harrowing.

My father listened to these reports with a grim expression. "They chose the more dangerous route," he said quietly one evening. "But they thought it gave them a better chance of reaching safety quickly. Who could have known?"

A New Home and New Challenges

As weeks turned into months, it became clear that we couldn't stay in Gornja Zenica indefinitely. My father, ever resourceful, began looking for better options. Eventually, he found a house closer to downtown Zenica, where a family was willing to rent out their renovated basement to refugees.

Moving day was a bittersweet milestone. While the promise of a more comfortable living space was exciting, I couldn't help but feel a pang of sadness leaving our little house in Gornja Zenica. That house, with its flower-lined path and the quirks of its eccentric communist owner, had become a haven during a tumultuous time. It was more than just a shelter; it was a place where we'd built memories, however modest.

Our new home was small—just two bedrooms, one bathroom, and a living room—but to us, it felt like a luxury. The upgrade was even more apparent when considering our circumstances: we now shared the space with my cousins from Štitkov Do. Their family of four and our family of three were crammed into the modest quarters. (Zilka and Selma had moved to live with their in-laws, who could offer more space, just before we left Gornja Zenica.) Despite the overcrowding, there was an unexpected comfort in being surrounded by family. After everything we'd endured, the closeness felt less like a burden and more like a balm for the soul.

Slowly, life began to take on a semblance of normalcy. I returned to school, though I was placed a grade behind to make up for the time I'd missed. The adjustment stung, but I was determined to catch up. My father, meanwhile, threw himself into whatever work he could find. Odd jobs and physical labor supplemented the small military pension he received. Each day, I watched him shoulder the weight of providing for us, his quiet determination a constant reminder of his resilience.

Though our new life was far from ideal, it was a start—a fragile foundation upon which we began rebuilding. The close quarters, the long hours of work, and even the challenges of adapting to a new routine felt insignificant compared to the sense of security we were slowly reclaiming.

A Surprise Trip

It was during this time that an unexpected opportunity arose. In my Islamic studies class at school, we were encouraged to read religious magazines provided by the Bosnian government. Each magazine contained a numbered coupon, and if you collected all 31, you could enter a drawing for prizes.

Despite our poverty, I was determined to enter. I carefully cut out each coupon, saving them in a makeshift envelope I'd crafted from a piece of paper and glue. When I had all 31, I addressed the envelope and sent it off, more out of a sense of completion than any real hope of winning.

Weeks later, as we were preparing for yet another move - this time to Sarajevo where my father had found better prospects - we received shocking news. Out of the entire country, only ten people had been selected for the grand prize - a trip to Turkey! And I was one of them.

The joy of winning was quickly tempered by reality. We had no money for a passport, let alone clothes or spending money for the trip. But my parents, seeing how much this meant to me, were determined to make it work.

The news got around our circle of friends and family and I got a scholarship. My father managed to request to expedite my passport application. My mother pieced together an outfit for me. And somehow, they scraped together a small amount of pocket money for the trip.

A moment captured in Istanbul, Turkey, in 1997.

As I prepared to leave for this unexpected adventure, I was struck by the contrast between this moment and the last time I'd left home for an unknown destination. Then, we had been fleeing for our lives. Now, I was embarking on a journey of discovery and learning. It felt like a reward for all we had endured, a sign that perhaps our fortunes were finally changing.

Little did I know that this trip would not only be an adventure but also a profound lesson in history and identity. As we traveled through Turkey in 1997, we visited villages that held a special significance for Bosniaks like myself. These were communities established by our ancestors who had fled Bosnia during the fall of the Ottoman Empire in the late 19th and early 20th centuries.

I learned that as the Ottoman Empire's grip on the Balkans weakened and the Austro-Hungarian Empire expanded its control, many Bosniak Muslims faced persecution and uncertainty. Fearing for their lives and their faith, they made the difficult decision to leave their homeland. They crossed continents, much like I had crossed war-torn landscapes, seeking safety and a place to practice their religion freely.

Walking through these villages, I was struck by the profound echoes of history. These were people who spoke my language, shared my customs, and practiced my faith, yet their connection to Bosnia had been severed over a century ago. Despite the distance and the passage of time, they had never forgotten their roots. They had built new lives in Turkey, but their identity as Bosniaks remained deeply ingrained, passed down through generations.

It reminded me of the struggle our people had faced to preserve that identity. Under the Kingdom of Yugoslavia and later the Yugoslav regime, the very name Bosniak was stripped from us in an attempt to erase our ethnicity. From 1909 to 1992, the term was banned, and replaced by labels meant to homogenize and diminish us. Yet, despite these efforts to erase who we were, the spirit of the Bosniak people endured, just as it had in these Turkish villages.

As I listened to the stories of these families, I couldn't help but reflect on the cyclical nature of history. Their journey mirrored my own in so many ways. They, too, had fled their homes, driven out by conflict and persecution, seeking safety and the freedom to live according to their beliefs. Standing there among them, I felt a deep kinship, as though their past and my present were threads of the same tapestry.

In those moments, I found myself grappling with questions about my future. Would my family and I, like these villagers, be forced to build a life far from our homeland? Would we, too, become part of a diaspora, preserving our identity and culture in a foreign land? Their resilience gave me hope, but it also left me with an aching uncertainty about what lay ahead.

Little did I know then that just three years after this visit, I would indeed follow in the footsteps of those long-ago Bosniak refugees. In 2000, my family and I would cross not just borders, but an entire ocean, settling in the United States. The reflections sparked by this trip to Turkey would become a reality sooner than I could have imagined.

This journey, won through a simple magazine contest, turned out to be so much more than a vacation. It was a window into my people's past and, unknowingly, a glimpse into my own future. It taught me about the resilience of identity, the long reach of history, and the unexpected ways our paths can mirror those of our ancestors.

Looking to the Future

As I boarded the bus that would take me to join the other winners for our trip to Turkey, I turned back for one last look at my parents. They stood arm in arm, proud smiles on their faces despite the worry I knew they must be feeling.

"Remember everything," my father called out. "So you can tell us all about it when you return."

I nodded, throat tight with emotion. As the bus pulled away, I pressed my face to the window, watching them until they faded from view. For the first time since leaving Žepa, I was traveling towards something, not away from it. It felt like the beginning of a new chapter, not just for me, but for our entire family.

The war had taken so much from us - our home, our sense of security, years of our lives. But as I settled into my seat, excitement building for the journey ahead, I realized it hadn't taken everything. We still had each other. We still had hope. And now, finally, we had a future to look forward to.

Our route to Turkey was anything but direct. Because of the recent war, we couldn't travel through Serbia. Instead, our bus had to take a long, winding path through Romania and Bulgaria before finally reaching Turkey. It was during this journey that we stopped in Sofia, the capital of Bulgaria, and I saw something I'll never forget.

As we pulled into Sofia, I was immediately struck by the buildings. They were old, Soviet-style structures that reminded me of the apartment blocks my grandmother used to live in back home. But what really caught my eye was what was in front of these buildings. There, parked neatly in rows, were countless cars - all identical except for their colors. It was like nothing I had ever seen before, a visual representation of life under Soviet influence that fascinated and perplexed me.

This stop in Sofia was more than just a break in our journey; it was a glimpse into a different world. Despite the obvious poverty - Bulgaria was struggling economically at the time - I found myself captivated by the differences and similarities to what I knew. It made me realize just how much there was to see and learn beyond the borders of my war-torn home.

As I traveled through these foreign lands, something profound began to stir within me. It was almost like a quick pill, a sudden realization that hit me unexpectedly. For the first time since the war, I began to see myself differently. I wasn't just a victim of circumstance anymore. I was a survivor, yes, but also an explorer, a witness to the world's vastness and diversity.

The sights, sounds, and experiences of this journey were awakening something in me. It was as if each mile we traveled, each new place we saw, was peeling away layers of pain and fear that the war had wrapped around me. I began to understand that I had been exposed to something extraordinary. My hardships, as terrible as they were, had also given me a unique perspective. I had seen the worst of humanity, but now I was seeing its resilience, its ability to rebuild and move forward.

Looking at the people in Sofia, and later in Turkey, I saw living proof of survival and prosperity. These were people whose ancestors had faced their own hardships, their own wars, and displacements, perhaps a hundred years ago or more. Yet here they were, living their lives, building their cities, raising their families. It was a powerful message to me: if they could survive and thrive after their hardships, couldn't I do the same?

This realization was like a spark of hope igniting in my chest. For the first time, I could envision a future beyond the war, beyond the refugee camps, beyond the constant fear and uncertainty. There was a whole world out there, full of possibilities. I might have lost my home, but I gained a broader perspective. I began to understand that my experiences, as painful as they were, could be a source of strength rather than just trauma.

The trip became more than just a journey across borders; it was a journey of self-discovery. I was no longer just a boy from a war-torn country. I was a survivor with a story to tell, with experiences that many others my age couldn't even imagine. And most importantly, I was someone with a future - a future that I could shape with my own hands, just as those before me had done.

This newfound perspective didn't erase the pain of what I'd been through, but it gave it meaning. It transformed my suffering into a tool for understanding the world and my place in it. I realized that I wasn't defined by what had happened to me, but by what I would choose to do with those experiences. The world was wide open, and for the first time since the war began, I felt a surge of excitement about what my future might hold.

CHAPTER 8

New Horizons

The Journey to Sarajevo

As the dust settled from our tumultuous exodus from Žepa, life in Zenica took on a semblance of routine. But for my family, it was clear that this was just another waypoint on our journey. In 1997, an opportunity arose that would once again uproot us, this time taking us to the heart of Bosnia – Sarajevo.

My father, ever resourceful, had managed to secure a small house on the outskirts of the capital. It wasn't much – similar to the humble dwelling we'd occupied in Gornja Zenica – but it represented a new beginning, a chance to be closer to family and potentially find better opportunities.

As we packed our meager belongings, I found myself filled with a mixture of excitement and apprehension. Sarajevo had always loomed large in my imagination – the grand capital city I'd visited as a child. But now, I knew we'd be facing a very different reality.

"What do you think it will be like, Babo?" I asked my father as we loaded our possessions onto a borrowed truck.

He paused, his face etched with both hope and concern. "It won't be easy, Adis," he said honestly. "The city has suffered greatly. But it's where we need to be. It's where we can start to rebuild our lives."

Arriving in a Wounded City

Our arrival in Sarajevo was a sobering experience. The city that had once been the jewel of Yugoslavia now lay battered and scarred, a stark testament to the longest siege of a capital city in modern warfare. For 1,425 days, from April 1992 to February 1996, Sarajevo endured a brutal blockade by the Army of Republika Srpska. The siege had been longer than the Battle of Stalingrad, longer even than the siege of Leningrad.

As we drove through the streets to our new home, I pressed my face against the window, trying to reconcile the Sarajevo of my childhood memories with the war-torn landscape before me. Bullet holes pockmarked buildings, windows were blown out, and entire blocks had been reduced to rubble. I learned later that at least 500,000 bombs had been dropped on the city during the siege. The destruction was a grim reminder of the price the city had paid for its resistance.

Despite the devastation, there was an energy to Sarajevo – people bustling about, small shops reopening, children playing in the streets. It was a city determined to live, to rebuild, to move forward. This resilience was all the more remarkable considering what the population had endured – months without gas, electricity, or water supply during the worst stages of the siege.

Our new home was modest – a small, old house on the outskirts of the city. But it was ours, at least for now, and it represented a new chapter in our lives. As we unloaded our few possessions, I caught my mother wiping away a tear.

"What's wrong, Majka?" I asked, concerned.

She smiled, though her eyes were still wet. "Nothing, Adis. It's just… we're here. We've made it this far. And now, maybe, we can start to think about the future."

I nodded, understanding the weight of her words. Sarajevo's population had been drastically reduced by the siege – from around 435,000 before the war to estimates between 300,000 and 380,000 after. We were part of this resilient remnant, determined to rebuild our lives in this wounded city.

As I helped unpack, I couldn't help but feel a mix of emotions – sadness for what had been lost, anger at the injustice of it all, but also a glimmer of hope. Sarajevo had survived its ordeal, and so had we. Now, like the city itself, it was time for us to start anew, to heal, and to look towards the future.

Starting Over… Again

Life in Sarajevo presented new challenges. My father, still officially part of the military, received a small pension, but it wasn't enough to sustain us. With characteristic determination, he found work as a newspaper delivery man for one of the city's publications.

Every morning before dawn, I'd hear him leave, his footsteps quiet so as not to wake us. He'd return hours later, having traversed the entire city on foot, his back bent from the weight of the papers he'd carried. Never once did I hear him complain.

One evening, as he sat resting his tired feet, I brought him a cup of coffee. "Is it very hard, Babo?" I asked, gesturing to his worn shoes.

He smiled, reaching out to ruffle my hair. "It's honest work, Adis. And it puts food on our table. That's what matters."

His resilience, and his unwavering commitment to providing for us, left a deep impression on me. It was a lesson in dignity and perseverance that I'd carry with me always.

Reconnecting with Family

One of the bright spots of our move to Sarajevo was the opportunity to reconnect with family members who had also gravitated to the capital. My grandmother, who had weathered the siege in the city, lived nearby, and for the first time since the war began, we were able to see her regularly.

I remember our first visit to her apartment building – a towering relic of Yugoslavia's socialist past. As we climbed the stairs (the elevator long since out of order), memories of childhood visits flooded back. The smell of her cooking, the sound of her laughter, the warmth of her embrace – it was all waiting for us at the top.

When she opened the door and saw us, tears sprang to her eyes. "My dear ones," she whispered, pulling us into a tight hug. "You're here. You're safe."

That afternoon, as we sat in her small living room, drinking coffee and eating the pita she'd prepared, I felt a sense of normalcy that had been absent for so long. It wasn't the life we'd had before the war, but it was a start.

Finding My Path on the Track

As I settled into life in Sarajevo and started at a new school, I found myself struggling to find my place. The gaps in my education due to the war were evident, and despite my best efforts, I often felt like I was falling behind.

It was during this time that a chance encounter would set me on a new path. One day during PE class, a man walked in and asked a simple question: "Who wants to join track and field?"

Something inside me stirred. I'd always been athletic, full of energy that often had nowhere to go. Without really thinking, I raised my hand.

The coach, noticing my enthusiasm, approached me after class. "Where are you from, boy?" he asked.

"Žepa," I replied, a hint of pride in my voice.

His eyes lit up. "Žepa! I knew a great athlete from there once. He trained with me on the Yugoslavian team." His face clouded for a moment. "He didn't make it through the war. But if you're half as talented as he was, you could go far."

That conversation was the beginning of a new chapter in my life. I joined the Athletic Club Bosna, and for the first time since leaving Žepa, I felt like I had found something that was truly mine.

Rising to the Challenge

Training was intense. Every day after school, I'd make my way to the track, pushing my body to its limits. The club didn't have much in the way of equipment or facilities – a legacy of the war – but what we lacked in resources, we made up for in determination.

I quickly discovered I had a talent for the decathlon – a grueling two-day event comprising ten different track and field disciplines. It was a test of not just physical ability, but mental toughness and versatility.

My parents, seeing how passionate I was about the sport, did everything they could to support me. My father, despite the long hours he worked and the physical toll of his job, always found the energy to encourage me.

"You're making us proud, Adis," he'd say, his eyes shining with a mix of pride and something else – hope, perhaps, for the future he saw opening up before me.

The cost of my training – a mere five marks a month – was a significant expense for our family. But my parents never complained, recognizing that this was more than just a sport for me. It was a lifeline, a way to reclaim some of the childhood that had been stolen by the war.

Breaking Records and Boundaries

As I threw myself into training, my skills improved rapidly. By 1998, I was competing at the national level, holding my own against athletes from all over Bosnia and Herzegovina.

The culmination of my efforts came when I set the national record for young juniors in the decathlon. Standing on the podium, hearing the national anthem play, I felt a surge of emotions – pride in my accomplishment, gratitude for the support of my family and coaches, and a deep sense of connection to my country.

This success opened new doors. In the summer of 1999, I was selected as part of a small group to travel to Hungary for a training camp. It was my second time leaving Bosnia since our flight from Žepa, and the prospect both thrilled and terrified me.

A Bittersweet Triumph

The trip to Hungary was eye-opening in many ways. As we crossed the border, I marveled at the intact buildings, and the smooth roads – all the little signs of a country untouched by recent war. It made me acutely aware of how much Bosnia had lost, and how far we had to go to rebuild.

Our training facility was near Budapest, and in our free time, we explored the city, wide-eyed at its beauty and vibrancy. It was during one of these excursions that tragedy struck. One of our teammates, diving into a lake, broke his neck. He would die in the hospital weeks later.

The bus ride back to Bosnia after the accident was somber, a stark contrast to the excited chatter that had filled the air on our journey there. As I watched the landscape roll by, I found myself grappling with profound questions about life, fate, and the fragility of human existence.

"How is it," I wondered, "that this boy survived the war, only to die here, on what should have been a joyful trip?"

It was a harsh reminder of the unpredictability of life, a lesson that would stay with me long after the details of the training camp had faded from memory.

Family Ties Stretched Across Oceans

As I was finding my footing in Sarajevo, our family was once again facing the prospect of separation. In 1997, Mubera and her husband received the opportunity to move to St. Louis, Missouri. The decision to go was difficult, tinged with both hope for a better future and sorrow at leaving us behind. The Bosnian community had established a thriving microcosm within St. Louis. There were Bosnian-owned businesses, cultural organizations, and even Bosnian language newspapers. The community had built several mosques, ensuring that we could continue our religious practices in our new home.

With an estimated 50,000 to 70,000 Bosnians calling the city home, St. Louis had become the largest Bosnian community outside of Bosnia itself. It was as if a piece of our homeland had been transplanted to the American Midwest.

As I am reflecting back years later when I visited St. Louis for the first time, what stuck with me the most about the Bosnian community was the unshakable sense of solidarity. Many shared stories eerily similar to ours—tales of war, loss, and the arduous journey of rebuilding a life in a foreign land. Yet, amid these painful memories, there was also a remarkable sense of hope and determination. Thousands of miles from our homeland, we were not just surviving but, in many ways, thriving. The community had created a space where our shared history became a source of strength, a foundation for new beginnings.

This sense of resilience was mirrored in the personal stories of our family. My sister Mubera's journey to motherhood is one such example. She and her husband had two children after the war—their eldest was born in 2003, eight years after the conflict ended, and their youngest arrived in 2008. Zilka, meanwhile, welcomed her son in 2002, born in the United States, reflecting yet another chapter of adaptation and new beginnings.

The timeline of Mubera's family reveals the deeper struggles our family faced in the aftermath of war. Her delayed start to motherhood wasn't merely a personal choice; it was a reflection of the profound hardships she and her husband endured. They battled fertility issues—a challenge that, though often hidden, is a common consequence of the stress and trauma that war inflicts on the body and spirit. Nearly eleven years of marriage passed before they were blessed with their first child, making the arrival of their children an extraordinary joy for our family.

In a way, their story is a testament to the strength and perseverance that defined our post-war life. Every child born into our family became a symbol of hope and renewal, a reminder that even in the aftermath of destruction, life has a way of blooming again.

The birth of Mubera's children marked a new chapter in our family's story. Unlike my older sister Zilka's children, who were born during or immediately after the war, Mubera's kids entered a world that was slowly healing. They represented hope and renewal for us, a sign that life was moving forward despite the hardships we had endured.

***

I remember the day they left, the airport a chaos of tearful goodbyes and anxious excitement. As I hugged Mubera, I whispered, "Don't forget us."

She squeezed me tight, her voice choked with emotion. "Never, Adis. We'll bring you all over as soon as we can."

Watching them disappear through the security gate, I felt a familiar ache – the pain of yet another separation. But this time, there was also a glimmer of hope. America represented possibility, a chance for a part of our family to build a new life free from the shadows of war.

A year later, that hope became a reality for another part of our family. My older sister Zilka, along with her husband and their two children – including little Elma, who was 2 years old, and had been born amidst the chaos of war – also received approval to emigrate to the United States.

The day of their departure was bittersweet. As we gathered in their small apartment, the air was thick with unspoken emotions. My mother, who had grown especially close to Selma during our time as refugees, struggled to maintain her composure.

"You'll call as soon as you arrive?" she asked Zilka, her voice wavering.

Zilka nodded, tears in her eyes. "Of course, Majka. And we'll start working on bringing you all over as soon as we can."

As we waved goodbye at the airport, watching another piece of our family fly off to a new life, I couldn't help but wonder: Would we be next? And if so, was I ready to leave behind the only home I'd ever known, damaged as it was?

The winds of change were blowing, carrying us towards an uncertain future. But for now, we remained in Sarajevo, clinging to the life we were slowly rebuilding, and to the hope that one day, our family would be whole again.

EPILOGUE

From Empty Wrappers to Full Circles

As I write these final words, I find myself reflecting on the journey that began with an empty chocolate wrapper and has led me to where I am today. The year 2000 marked not just the turn of a millennium, but a turning point in my life – the year my family and I arrived in the United States, carrying little more than our hopes and the weight of our experiences.

Landing in America was like stepping into a world I had only dreamed of, a stark contrast to the war-torn landscapes of my childhood. The abundance of everything, from food to opportunities, was overwhelming at first. I remember standing in a grocery store, marveling at the rows upon rows of chocolate bars – no longer just empty wrappers, but tangible symbols of a new life filled with possibilities.

But the transition wasn't without its challenges. Learning a new language, adapting to a new culture, and carrying the invisible scars of war – these were hurdles that required resilience and determination to overcome. Yet, it was precisely the hardships I had endured that gave me the strength to face these new challenges head-on.

Contrary to what one might expect, the terrible experiences of war did not slow me down. Instead, they became the fuel that propelled me forward. The lessons of perseverance, adaptability, and appreciation for life's simple pleasures that I had learned in the most difficult circumstances now served as the foundation for building a new life.

Education became my passport to a brighter future. I threw myself into my studies with the same intensity that had once been reserved for survival. Each book I read, and each concept I mastered felt like a victory not just for myself, but for all those who had sacrificed to give me this opportunity. The empty wrapper of my past was gradually being filled with knowledge, understanding, and purpose.

Sports, which had once been a luxury in times of war, became another avenue for growth and self-expression. The discipline and teamwork I had learned in the most dire circumstances translated well to the playing field. Each victory, each personal best was a testament to the resilience of the human spirit.

As I progressed through my education and into my professional career, I found that my unique perspective – shaped by war but not defined by it – was an asset. The ability to find solutions in scarce resources, to persevere in the face of adversity, and to appreciate every opportunity became the cornerstones of my success. From entry-level positions to roles of increasing responsibility, I carried with me the lessons learned from empty wrappers and the value of every small victory.

But perhaps the most significant growth has been intellectual and mental. The experiences of my childhood, while traumatic, have given me a depth of understanding and empathy that I might not have otherwise developed.

They've instilled in me a drive to make the most of every opportunity, to give back to my community, and to work towards a world where no child has to experience what I did.

As I look back on the journey from that young boy holding an empty chocolate wrapper to the man I am today, I'm filled with a profound sense of gratitude. Gratitude for the resilience of my family, for the sacrifices of those who didn't survive, for the kindness of strangers who became friends, and for the opportunities that have allowed me to turn trauma into triumph.

But this is not the end of the story. In many ways, it feels like just the beginning. The empty wrapper of my past has been filled with experiences, achievements, and growth, but there are still many chapters to be written. Perhaps another book lies in the future – one that delves deeper into the process of rebuilding a life after war, reconciling past and present, and using our most challenging experiences as stepping stones to a brighter future.

Thank you for accompanying me on this journey. May your own story, whatever it may be, be one of resilience, growth, and unwavering belief in the power of the human spirit to overcome even the darkest of times.

As you close this book, I encourage you to look at your own 'empty wrappers' – those challenges or voids in your life that seem insurmountable. Our past does not define us; it merely provides the wrapper. It is up to us to fill it with the richness of a life well-lived.

About The Author

Adis Ziga is a Bosnian-American author and professional currently residing in Charlotte, North Carolina. Born in 1983 in Žepa, Bosnia and Herzegovina, Adis survived the Bosnian War as a child before immigrating to the United States in 2000. Prior to his departure, he achieved a significant athletic milestone, setting the Bosnian National Record for younger juniors in decathlon as a member of Athletic Club "Bosna".

Upon arriving in the US, Adis pursued his education at Catawba College, earning a Bachelor of Business Administration degree. After graduation, he began his career in the Banking Industry, where he has worked for 13 years.

Drawing from his experiences during the war and as an immigrant, Adis has become an advocate for the Bosnian diaspora and various humanitarian causes. He has been actively involved in organizing events and educating fellow Bosnians on voter registration and participation in Bosnian elections. His volunteer work extends to assisting individuals with translation, supporting Habitat for Humanity, and serving at local homeless shelters and soup kitchens.

Adis has also been affiliated with a nonprofit organization, helping clients with personal self-development, small business and entrepreneurial development, and lifestyle coaching. His commitment to community service and personal growth reflects the resilience and determination that have characterized his life journey.

When not writing or working, Adis enjoys working out, reading, spending time with his family, traveling, collecting old coins, and geeking out on history. His memoir, "The Empty Chocolate Wrapper," is his first book, offering a powerful and personal account of childhood during war and the journey of rebuilding life in a new country. Through his writing and community involvement, Adis continues to bridge cultures and inspire others with his story of perseverance and hope.

www.ingramcontent.com/pod-product-compliance
Lightning Source LLC
Chambersburg PA
CBHW070142080526
44586CB00015B/1799